101 More Improv Games for Children and Adults

Praise for 101 More Improv Games

"Bob has been a popular staple of the Utah theatre scene for many years. His improv and acting instruction is stellar and students leaving his workshop room are always energized and excited to go out and practice what they just learned. His sense of humor and ability to relate to young people are parts of what make him so popular. He gets participants up on their feet and DOING what he is teaching them. He has a great ability to side-coach and encourage actors so that they are making choices and discovering the creative process alongside creating a fantastic product."

— Shawnda Moss
Brigham Young University Theatre Education Faculty
Utah Theatre Association Board of Directors

"In addition to being an important part of my development as a performer, improvisation has given me skills that continue to serve me every day of my life. The ability to problem solve, embrace uncertainty, and work together with others are just a few of improv's benefits. All of these skills and more blend perfectly in Bob, who is a brilliant instructor, performer, and human being. I'm privileged to have worked with him on a number of occasions and cannot recommend his work or his knowledge highly enough. BUY THIS BOOK!"

— Hal Lublin
The Thrilling Adventure Hour
thrillingadventurehour.com

T0151291

SmartFun Activity Books from Hunter House

101 Music Games for Children by Jerry Storms

101 More Music Games for Children by Jerry Storms

101 Dance Games for Children by Paul Rooyackers

101 More Dance Games for Children by Paul Rooyackers

101 Movement Games for Children by Huberta Wiertsema

101 Drama Games for Children by Paul Rooyackers

101 More Drama Games for Children by Paul Rooyackers

101 Improv Games for Children by Bob Bedore

101 Language Games for Children by Paul Rooyackers

101 Life Skills Games for Children by Bernie Badegruber

101 More Life Skills Games for Children by Bernie Badegruber

101 Cool Pool Games for Children by Kim Rodomista

101 Family Vacation Games by Shando Varda

101 Relaxation Games for Children by Allison Bartl

101 Pep-Up Games for Children by Allison Bartl

101 Quick-Thinking Games + Riddles for Children by Allison Bartl

404 Deskside Activities for Energetic Kids by Barbara Davis, MA, MFA

Yoga Games for Children by Danielle Bersma and Marjoke Visscher

The Yoga Adventure for Children by Helen Purperhart

The Yoga Zoo Adventure by Helen Purperhart

Yoga Exercises for Teens by Helen Purperhart

101 Circus Games for Children by Paul Rooyakers

303 Preschooler-Approved Exercises and Active Games by Kimberly Wechsler

303 Kid-Approved Exercises and Active Games by Kimberly Wechsler

303 Tween-Approved Exercises and Active Games by Kimberly Wechsler

101 More Improv Games for Children and Adults by Bob Bedore

101 <u>More</u> Improv Games for Children and Adults

THE IMPROVISERS

all of your favorites!

Bob Bedore

Illustrated by Trevor Robertson

A Hunter House SmartFun Book

DEDICATION

I want to dedicate this book to Russ McBride, an actor whom I was privileged not only to share the stage with many, many times but also to call a very dear friend. He had an ability to connect with an audience in a way that very few can, and he will be greatly missed. Much of what I teach in improv comes from spending time with him and just trying to catch up. I will continue to live up to the standards that Russ brought to the stage and will look forward to the time we can perform together again.

Hunter House Inc., Publishers
PO Box 2914
Alameda CA 94501-0914

Library of Congress Cataloging-in-Publication Data
Bedore, Bob.
101 more improv games for children and adults / Bob Bedore.
pages   cm
Includes index.
ISBN 978-0-89793-652-1 (trade paper) —ISBN 978-0-89793-654-5 (spiral)
ISBN 978-0-89793-653-8 (ebook)
1. Improvisation (Acting) 2. Games. I. Title. II. Title: One hundred one more improv games.   III. Title: One hundred and one more improv games.
PN2071.I5B445 2013
792.02′8—dc23   2012048651

Project Credits

Cover Design: Jinni Fontana	Special Sales Manager: Judy Hardin
Book Production: John McKercher	Rights Coordinator: Candace Groskreutz
Developmental and Copy Editor: Amy Bauman	Publisher's Assistant: Bronwyn Emery
Managing Editor: Alexandra Mummery	Customer Service Manager: Christina Sverdrup
Editorial Intern: Jordan Collins	Order Fulfillment: Washul Lakdhon
Acquisitions Intern: Sally Castillo	Administrator: Theresa Nelson
Publicity Coordinator: Martha Scarpati	IT Support: Peter Eichelberger
Publisher: Kiran S. Rana	

Manufactured in the United States of America

First Edition

Contents

A list of the games, divided by age groups, begins on the next page. Please note that the illustrations in this book are all outline drawings. The fact that the pages are white does not imply that the people all have white skin. This book is for people of all races and ethnic identities.

List of Games

Acknowledgments

While I've been doing improv nearly every week for twenty years, I've hardly been doing it alone. I want to thank all the wonderful actors who have taught me so much about the importance of teamwork when it comes to improv. There are far too many of you to mention, but each of you has helped make me a better improviser and person.

And a big thanks to my illustrator, Trevor Robertson. Little did I know that this talented improviser and actor was so good with art. Check out his other works!

I also want to thank Mary Mason and my daughter, Briana Bedore, for reading over various drafts and helping me pick which games should be in this book. They were both invaluable to getting it done.

And lastly I want to thank Hunter House Publishers for letting me express my love of improv in these books and hopefully instill at least a little of it in you. I need to thank those doing the nearly thankless job of editing my ramblings. When I teach I get a little worked up and my thoughts are all over the place, but the team at Hunter House helped compact everything into its now-usable form. Alex Mummery, Amy Bauman, Jordan Collins, Martha Scarpati, and anyone else who put their eyes to this before printing... I owe you much thanks!

Introduction

Getting Started

So here it is, a second book on improv and another lists of games to play and enjoy. Just like my first book, I want to point out that there is no "Bible of Improv." It's not a science that you can break down into exact equations for success. It is an art, and everyone will have an opinion. If you are truly excited about improv, I would suggest reading everything you can find on it and viewing as many troupes and forms as you can.

That's how I came to my views on the subject. I went to classes and performances all over the country. I have played with more troupes than I can possibly remember, and I've tried to keep everything fresh for almost nineteen years. I still perform every week and still love it.

This book is more of a continuation of the first. If you're looking for exact methods for teaching children how to do improv, I'd suggest that you start with the first book. There I've outlined a curriculum that you can follow with newcomers. The games in that book are also a little more suited to people who are just starting out and exploring improv. And while you'll find plenty of fun games for newbies in this book, too, I've tried to stretch a bit more this time and include some harder games and even a full section on long-form improv.

I believe that improv (and all theater arts) can be very important to young and old alike. It instills confidence in people and makes them less afraid to face life's challenges. Sure that may seem a little verbose, but I've seen it time and time again. I use improv in the corporate world to teach people how to adapt to situations and to perform as a team. The rules that we follow in improv are no different from those you'd want the people around you to follow: Listen, treat everyone as an equal, be involved, and stay focused.

If at any point you have a question about anything in this book, or improv in general, I invite you to e-mail me at bob@quickwitscomedy.com. It is my goal to give you a very satisfying improv experience.

Back to the Basics

Okay, so the title of the book has the word *More* in it, so I'm guessing that it's safe to assume that you know that it's a second book. I'm hoping that you picked up the first book, *101 Improv Games for Children and Adults*, and already read my thoughts on the basic rules of improv. (I can wait if you want to do that now.) But just in case you're new to improv and need a little tip as to what to do, or maybe just want a refresher, here you go.

First off, yes, improv is making things up. But it's a lot more than that. Improv is a creation of scenes—full scenes. It's not just a random mess of thoughts. Improv is also a great exercise in teamwork and is a wonderful way to build confidence in people of all ages.

I'll go into much of that later, but let's talk about the basics of improv. In improv, people are given a situation and must act their way through it. There is no script for this task, and it's somewhat like jumping out of a plane without knowing if there is a parachute in your pack. There is a lot of trust and hope involved, and you usually experience some frantic moments until you know you're safe and can relax and enjoy the ride.

And learning to do improv is a lot like learning to swim. It's easiest to just get thrown in and start trying to do it. Survival instincts kick in at some point, and you figure things out quickly. Or you learn that this isn't for you and move on to something else. Luckily in improv you can just get off the stage. The swimming example could lead to a much worse outcome.

Rules? Do We Really Need Rules? Yes, and…No

You can look up *improv* on the Internet and find all sorts of ways to get started and to learn what to do, but one of the things you'll be sure to run into is the "Rules of Improv." And what the rules will say is things like, "use 'Yes, and,'" "Don't ask questions," "Don't say 'No,'" and some other things that every improviser must comply with in order to perform well.

I'm not so worried about those things. I want my players just to be in the moment and not worry about the rules. I call this "being on stage instead of in your head." I have often found that players who just go with the flow of the scene are going to do things naturally and that usually takes care of the rules. Those who are thinking too much about what they should or shouldn't do in a scene have lost touch with what is going on around them.

But the rules do include some good points. The idea of saying "Yes, and" and not saying "No" really apply to making sure that you accept the reality of what you have been given. If someone says that you are in a submarine, that's it; you're in a submarine. It's been established, and you have to go with it. It doesn't mean that you can't leave the sub at some point in the scene, but it does mean that you have to work with it for the time being.

But that's not a bad thing. For many people, it takes the pressure off. Now everyone can just roll with what has been set in motion and make their way through the scene.

Now although I don't want people concentrating on the "rules," I do have some guidelines that I think are important. First and foremost, I want all actors to respect each other. I look at every actor I'm on stage with as if he or she is the best possible person I could share this scene with, and I want that person to do the same with me. Are there times when I'm on stage with someone who I know isn't the best? Yes, it happens. But the key is treating each actor as if he is the best and working with him, not trying to just "save" the scene. (I'll talk about this later.)

Another thing: Don't try to be funny. I know; that's a strange thing to say when we're talking about a comedy show. But the hidden part of that goes back to the above paragraphs. If you are trying to be funny, you're not working through a scene.

In short, keep your eyes and ears open. This is the big reason for being "on stage" mentally. Watching and listening to everything that is happening on stage is very important to being a team player. If you're thinking about some great line that you're about to say, you might just miss some key information. Your team is counting on you to keep things going, and you might have just messed that up. You might say that it's improv, and you're just supposed to go with it, and you'd be right. But be a team player in all that you do.

Improv Is Easy; Just Don't Tell Anyone

So really, improv is easy. It's like walking, but instead of one foot in front of the other, you're doing one line after another. As boring as that might sound, by doing all of these things, you will create magic. I guarantee it. And you'll also find that it will be funny.

What I've tried to lay out is just the groundwork. The first book, *101 Improv Games for Children and Adults,* offered more of the basics, and you can find guidelines for improv all over the place. There is no science to what takes place; there is no "one way" to do it right. Study from all you can find and then develop your style. I've been doing this for twenty years, and I still read everything I can find about it and attend every class I can. There is always more to learn…which is why there are more chapters in this book before we get to the games!

Making a
Scene Work

I take comedy improv very seriously. I have a lot of fun and love making people laugh, but it's just as important to me that I am doing a scene. This may seem strange when you're playing a game like "Mousetraps" (covered later in this book), but no matter how gimmicky a game may seem, it needs to have a scene to really make it work.

Improv should look like it's part of a staged play that we've spent weeks rehearsing. The same elements that go into those scenes need to go into your improv: character work, realism, conflict, and resolution. I'll go into how to build a strong character later, but let's look at how we can build on the other elements now.

Base Your Scenes in Reality

My first concern is that the scene starts off in something "real." It doesn't have to end there (and usually doesn't), but it needs to start there. The audience needs to feel connected to a scene for it to work, and starting with something very normal allows them to do that. Just as important, it gives you a launching pad to take off into the wacky side of things. If you start already crazy, you've got nowhere to go, and you've probably lost the audience.

Here's an example. I was about to start a scene with a new actor, and we were given "knitting" as our setup. The first words he said as I came on stage were, "Alright, Granny, are you ready to knit to the death?" I liked the energy, but, without a buildup, the scene didn't have a place to go. Things can escalate quickly, but they still need a starting point. In this scene, I laughed off his comment and let him know that it was time to start his lesson. We worked the scene for a little while before I stabbed him with the needles, proclaiming that I was the winner and that he'd fallen for the oldest trick in the book.

The point is, start normal, then ramp things up.

Practice the Art of Conflict

Conflict. I've worked with instructors who hate conflict in scenes. They feel that it is a cheap way to get a scene going, but I feel that conflict is such a normal part of everyday life that it's unavoidable, so you might as well use it to help you in a scene.

Conflict doesn't always involve people with opposing views. It doesn't mean that there is going to be a fight. It just means that a scene is something more than just two people agreeing with each other all the time—even in a scene where everyone is happy and agreeing all the time.

Let's look at a scene about a guy who is going to propose marriage to his girlfriend, and she has been waiting to say "Yes" for a long time. While that seems like a conflict-free scene, it won't make for a good scene.

So try adding just a little conflict. The guy can't find the ring. Someone at the next table is being loud. Our guy is not asking quickly enough for the girl. He's nervous. The ring doesn't fit. The power goes out. There is a zombie invasion! Any one of these occurrences adds conflict and makes the story a little more interesting.

Resolve the Conflict

Once the conflict is set, you can work to resolve it. The great thing is that the people you're on stage with likely know the conflict you are having and can work with it. If you don't think they have it, let them know! Sometimes you have to be obvious and spell it out. The resolution won't work if everyone is on different pages.

The resolution is important for a few reasons. One is the audience. They will want to see what happens. They will want to know if the proposal goes well. People like things wrapped up. Another reason is that it will help give an ending to a scene. Not all improv scenes will end on a resolve (often they'll end on a big laugh), but the resolve is a great place to end.

To move to a resolution, characters just have to move through things. The flow of things will still get to the proper ending. For instance, we want the couple to get married, so no matter what happens we know the finish line. Keeping that goal in sight will help push the scene to it—even in a zombie apocalypse.

Add the Third Actor

I'm not sure how it started, or why it's become fairly universal, but most scenes will start with two actors, and then a third will be introduced by either coming on stage or being called to the stage.

The reason for this is that this third actor can do a lot for a scene. She can come in and raise the bar with new information, he can create or resolve a conflict, she can get a scene back on track if it has strayed or do any other number of things to give a scene what it needs. An experienced improviser can be just off stage, feel what is needed, and come out at the exact right moment to make an impact.

New players and troupes will want to get as much stage time as possible, and I'll see scenes start with four or more people from the beginning, but I want you to think about waiting off stage. You'll find that coming in for the last half of the scene is often more powerful than being in it from the beginning.

Creating Your Character and Your World

In improv, a simple acronym can help you keep everything in perspective: CROW. This stands for **c**haracter (who you are), **r**elationship (how you react to others), **o**bjective (what you want), and **w**here (the world/environment where the scene takes place).

It is actually pretty simple to create scenes in both long- and short-form improv by keeping these details in place. Take a moment before the scene begins to determine an answer for all four. Knowing them will help guarantee a successful scene.

Give Life to Your Character

Most improvisers start out being pretty much themselves on stage. That is perfectly fine. Improv is about having confidence in what you do, and being yourself will certainly help with that. The only problem is that things could get stale for you very quickly.

This is where creating a character will come in handy. A character who is not your normal self will answer questions differently from how you might. He or she will feel differently about various subjects. Creating a character allows you to be someone else for a while, and isn't that why most of us got into theater?

Instant Character Creation

So how do you create a character quickly? The simple answer is to pick one thing that will be that character's motivation. Let's say that your motivation is money. Everything you do in that scene should reflect on how your actions will bring you money. And it's best if that motivation is something different from your real persona.

Some people are naturally gifted at characters. They can do voices, change up their bodies, and do things that transform them. For whatever reason, I don't do that very much. I stick to the simple things, and they work for me.

Character Movement

Another thing that can help you in improv (and any form of theater) is how you move. This is another great way to give our character some different levels. When I teach improv classes, I often spend an entire day on movement. My choice is always the Laban Method.

A Laban Method Movement Analysis (see the example in the table below) shows that movement can define a character. It looks at the effort in movement as it relates to space, weight, and time. It asks some questions about your character. Is your movement direct or indirect, strong or light, sudden or sustained? The different answers to each of these can be summed up with one word as seen in the chart below.

A Sample Laban Method Movement Analysis

Space	Weight	Time	Identifier
Direct	Strong	Sudden	Punch (Thrust)
Indirect	Strong	Sudden	Slash
Direct	Strong	Sustained	Push
Indirect	Strong	Sustained	Wring
Direct	Light	Sudden	Dab
Indirect	Light	Sudden	Flick
Direct	Light	Sustained	Glide
Indirect	Light	Sustained	Float

So, what does this all mean? Take a look at the word *punch*. A character moving as a "punch" is going to move in a direct, strong, and sudden manner... like a punch. This is going to be a very strong character. The word *direct* shows that the movement is focused. Contrast that with *slash*, which is indirect, like a sword strike. Both are strong characters; one is just more direct.

If you work with this method long enough, you can call out a word and tell a lot about the character. Take a moment and think about the type of character that would be a "float." He is "indirect" so the character has no focus. He is "light," so he doesn't have much force. And he is "sustained," meaning that he takes his time. This character is basically the human version of a balloon, so the term *float* fits well.

Each word fits a character type, so it's easy just to say, "I'm going to be a 'flick' in this scene," and you've got a whole new character.

Set the Stage

Creating a living, breathing world in which to set your scene will help make it work. I know that it's not easy in a black box setup with limited props and scenery, but it can be done.

One of the first things you have to do is see the world. Don't just look at a blank stage and pretend that it's a kitchen. See the kitchen. Know where every appliance, cabinet, and drawer is located. Take a moment to visualize the setting and then act in it.

Simple Actions Lead to Great Results

You don't have to be an expert in mime for this to work. Simple things like reaching into a cabinet for a bowl before cracking eggs into it will make a huge difference. Soon the audience will be right there in the kitchen with you.

And the things you bring in also have a way of giving you more to do. I often use an example of sitting at a desk and pushing a button to call my assistant to say I'm ready for my next appointment. With that simple action, I establish a lot. I must be important to have an assistant. I have another room outside of this one, so I've just doubled my stage size. I have announced at least two characters (the assistant and the next appointment, which could be more than one person).

Taking a moment to think about your surroundings is a simple gesture, but it has so much behind it. Opening a window on stage says there is a whole world out there. I've done scenes where we moved to the ledge of a building to avoid others hearing us. Take the audience on a ride with your scene. Don't only play it out in your head.

Remember What You Create

Later in this book, you'll see a game called "Swing Shift." One of the reasons this game was developed was for people to really have to pay attention to the environment that was being created. You can use this as a workshop game to teach people about creating worlds.

Don't Be Afraid to Change Your Location

One difficulty of short-form improv is that the scenes are so short and you don't have time to go to many locations. But there are ways around that.

I already brought up the meeting I held on a ledge. That was one way to move to a location. We simply climbed out the window and inched our way across the ledge. Now we had much more to work with than a generic business-meeting scene. We even had the assistant come out, take notes, and get some coffee.

I've seen other scenes change when someone opens a vortex to another place, uses a time machine, or tries other methods of teleportation. I call this the "Narnia Effect." It can be a simple way to shift your scene quickly and effectively.

Improv Magic Moment #1: The Effective Exit

One thing I love about improv is that I can always learn something. One night I was doing a show with a local ComedySportz troupe. In one scene, two people were discussing how one of them wasn't feeling well. One actor suggested they go to the doctor, and they quickly exited.

In a blink of an eye, the third actor came on stage, and the first two came back through the door, now acting as if they were at the hospital. It was so simple and so magical. I couldn't believe I hadn't done that before. It was nothing more than leaving a scene and establishing a new one.

Since then I've used this trick often. With it, you can go anywhere in a blink of an eye. I've also used it to make time pass, saying something like, "I'll be back in two hours; you'd better be finished." I then make a quick exit and return, announcing, "Your two hours are up."

Improv Magic Moment #2: The Car Chase

During an improvised musical one night, the scene started to work its way into a car chase. Two actors sat in chairs (their car) and another actor, playing a police officer, got into another car and gave chase. He pulled over the first car, and as he started going through the whole "license and registration" thing, the other actor threw his license at the officer and drove off.

The officer began running after the car, which remained just out of reach. Keep in mind that this was all being mimed; they really weren't going anywhere. The actor ran for about twenty seconds before realizing that he needed his car. He then turned and ran back to his car. Yes, the chair was right next to him, but he realized that if he'd run for a while in one direction, he'd better run back.

Team Play

Improv has to be about trust. It's all about confidence that your team will be with you and will help you out on stage. It's not about being a star.

This example might not ring with everyone right away, but if you've ever seen the Harlem Globetrotters, you'll know what I mean. (And if you haven't seen them, watch a video of them doing their signature routine to the song "Sweet Georgia Brown.")

The team gathers in a circle at center court, and everyone passes the basketball around while the music plays. The ball goes from one player to the next, with each person taking a moment to do something with it before passing it on. No player acts as if he is the star of the team. And the other players do not seem jealous about not having the ball. They are all just enjoying the moment.

And the goal of what they are doing? The goal is simply to keep the ball moving, keep it from hitting the ground, and wait for their moment with the ball—letting it come to them and not going after it at the cost of the others. This is what team improv is all about.

Learn about Your Team

When working with others, remember my rule about treating every actor as if he or she is the perfect actor to have in the scene with you. One of the best approaches to making that true is to talk to the performers you're working with. Ask them what they like to do, what their hobbies are, etc. Finding out something about them will help you work with them.

On the other side, if actors ask you what games you like to play, saying "I like anything," may make you sound like a great player, but it doesn't help the other actors. They want to know what games will help you feel at your best. So for now, answer the question, because they are trying to help you; later you can show them that you can play anything.

A while back, one actor in our troupe was having trouble fitting in. Other members talked about how we needed to cut him. I had to agree that it wasn't working out. But then a strange thing happened. We took his incredible knowledge of history and war and brought that to the stage. Once he was in an area where he felt comfortable and could shine, he was able to move that to all forms of improv. Soon, his confidence grew, and, with that, the troupe's confidence in him grew, too. He is now one of the best improvisers in the state.

Always Be in the Show

Be in the game all the time. Even when you're not playing, you can watch and be engaged in the scene. You never know when an opportunity to join a scene might come up. And actors who tune out when they're not playing give the impression that they care only when it involves them. That's not what makes a team.

Many shows have actors on stage even when they are not playing. Some actors will forget that little point—that they're "on stage"—and begin pulling focus by doing things that seem normal. But such actions are normal only when you're not in the middle of a stage. Even if you're just sitting there thinking about something unrelated, you might have a bored look on your face. People in the audience will see that and instantly think less of the scene they are watching.

Remember: If you are on stage and can be seen by the audience, you are in the show.

Find Your Fit

If you are interested in joining a troupe, go and see that group's shows. You can learn a lot about a troupe by watching the actors on stage. You'll see the type of show they perform—for example, whether they are big on physical, musical, or long form or play with crazy gimmicks—and you'll be able to tell if it's something that suits you.

You will also see how the actors react with each other. Some troupes, for example, are obviously a group of friends. These are tough groups to break into because they have a lot of private jokes and common history that will make you feel like an outsider. I recommend hanging out with these people for a while before actually getting on stage. Gathering some information on the various members of the troupe will help you know how best to work with them. And if you don't learn about them, you might be left out of a scene just like in real life. You might be able to do improv as good, or better, than anyone on that troupe, but those little inside jokes will always trip you up.

I started the troupe "Quick Wits" back in 1994, and we've enjoyed a lot of success locally, while touring, and from a brief dabble with television. One thing that sets us apart from many troupes is that we are more like a dysfunctional family. Anything about us is fair game for comedy. For example, a tall, skinny player will get a lot of jokes about that. Same with nationality, still living at home, dating disasters, etc. We kid each other all the time and then bring that on stage during a show. We've found that it works well with our audience, and they feel like they're a part of us.

But that type of personal humor doesn't work in all troupes. I've made the mistake of not finding out about the type of people I'm playing with and how they like to perform. It's a mistake I no longer make. I also make sure to warn everyone one who comes into Quick Wits about our style.

Improv Magic Moment #3: NASCAR Ballet

I've seen many examples of great teamwork over the years, but this one will stick with me forever. It involved actors Jourdan Dixon, Brittney Nielson, and Blake Heywood. The game was "Ballet," in which actors have to perform a ballet about a strange subject. The subject was NASCAR.

It started with Blake and Brittney dancing to solidify their love. This *pas de deux* involved sharing a drink from his "two can beer hat" and a dance of pure joy. When Jourdan came on the scene as a stud NASCAR driver, he immediately stole Brittney's heart. A rejected Blake danced his way off stage to the loudest "Aww" I've ever heard from a crowd.

The new lovers danced a *pas de deux* of their own inside Jourdan's car, during the race. Unfortunately their love caused a crash, setting the car and Jourdan on fire. Brittney danced as she tried to put out the flames. In the background, Blake came back on stage with binoculars and a gun. As the crowd roared, Brittney pleaded with him to help with the fire, but instead, Blake sadly danced his way over to them, shot them, and then shot himself.

Sure the ending was dark, but it was true to the tragic ballet formula, the actors were in sync, and the crowd cheered for longer than the game actually took.

Guessing Games

Later in this book, you'll see a section of games called "Guessing Games." They're great games to play because the audience can play along with you. They are in on the answer and get to watch an actor struggle to figure out the clue—and that can lead to big laughs.

It's Not Charades; It's a Scene

First, remember that all of these are scenes. All the elements of a good scene should be found in all guessing games. Let's take the game "Late for Work" (Game #70 from *101 Improv Games for Children and Adults*) as an example. In this game, one actor is late for work and is sure to be fired unless he can come up with good reasons for being late. A coworker tries to help him by feeding him reasons (retrieved from the audience) without his boss knowing.

That last part is the key. Without the boss on stage, the game is nothing more than charades. By adding an element of a "boss" and trying to keep him in the dark, we now have a scene. The boss is now someone that the guesser has to communicate with all while trying to figure out the clues from the coworker.

This scene creation should run through any game that involves someone having to guess an endowment or some item. Having to do this guessing in the context of an actual scene is what makes things interesting.

Improv Magic Moment #4: Late for the Death Star

I don't like to put myself in a "Magical Moment," but I love how perfectly this scene fit together. It revolved around the game "Late for Work" (see above) where one employee is about to get fired unless he can come up with a good reason for being late. Luckily the employee has a friend who is helping him come up with reasons, all while keeping it from the boss.

As the "late for work" guy, I came on stage to find out the place I was working was the Death Star. Immediately a light went off in my head. I told the boss

(Drew Keddington) that I was sorry I was late and that I wanted to get right to work closing the exhaust port. Drew told me that first he wanted me to explain why I was late. I said I would explain as soon as I closed the exhaust port, but he refused. Drew knew exactly where I was going with this.

Meanwhile Jason Wild, the actor giving me clues, gave me my first reason for being late: my alarm didn't go off. I added that it didn't go off because some crazy guy had broken through our security and shut down the power to half of the station, including my room and alarm clock. I could hardly be blamed for the base's poor security. I wanted to close the exhaust port but was again told "No," so I needed to give another excuse.

The second excuse was that Godzilla had gone on a rampage, causing a huge mess. Since I hadn't been stomped, Drew pointed out, I shouldn't have been late. I explained that I had to clean up the mess and that the trash compactor was broken; it turned out that some huge piece of metal was blocking it. Drew talked about a memo about people needing to separate their trash before putting it into the compactor. Still he wouldn't let me close the port.

Along the way we made every *Star Wars* reference we could, including talking about a new restaurant that opened up in the food court called the E-Wok. The three of us are all nerds; it was easy and fun. Finally I gave a third reason and was told I could close the hatch. Just as I reached for it, we all reacted to a big explosion. My being late had allowed the rebels to destroy the Death Star.

As I said, Guessing Games are scenes, not charades.

Musical Games

Musical games are magical in the world of improv. People think that coming up with lines of dialogue is hard to do, but when you do it while making the lines rhyme and following a tune, you've really done something strong.

The very last game in this book goes through steps of how to create an entire improvised musical. It's like magic times magic, and is literally the most fun I've ever had doing improv, possibly because it is so frightening.

Performing musical improv is incredibly rewarding, and audiences will eat it up, but it can be very hard to pull off. That is why I suggest sticking to some simple rules.

Less Is More, and It's Easier

First thing to keep in mind is that there is no shame in brevity. I've seen many people try to put too much into their songs. Look at the songs of today; many have fewer words than a Dr. Seuss book, and often with the same sort of rhymes.

The fewer words you use, the less chance that you'll mess them up. Keep in mind that your cleverness will come through in moving things along, telling some sort of story, and getting some rhymes.

Work from the Bottom Up

I wait until I hear the topic of my song and then start to make a mental list of everything I might discuss within that topic. I do this quickly, keeping all the words that are easy to rhyme.

Most songs will have some sort of rhyming scheme. The most common will be ABCB. This means that in four lines of lyrics, the last word in line four will rhyme with the last word in line two. Lines one and three will not end in a rhyme; that's why we have an "A" and a "C." Here is an ABCB scheme:

Roses are red,
Violets are blue,
Sugar is sweet,
And so are you.

I always think backward, figuring out the last word of any phrase first. I'll make it the easiest word to rhyme on my list. Then I'll choose the word I want to use as the rhyming word and put that in place as the end of the second line.

For example, if I am doing a love song about plumbing (for some reason that always comes up), I start to think about words that fit that profession: toilet, drain, plunger, snake, clog, sink, pipe…. The list includes a few good rhyming words, but if *My Fair Lady* has taught me anything, it's that the "ain" sound is easy to rhyme. I'll go with *drain*.

Now I know I'm ending with *drain,* and I want an easy word to rhyme it with, so I'll take "pain" (and you can't have a true love song without talking about pain). Now we just throw the image together and come up with some lyrics:

When you left me, my heart just stopped.
My pipes were bursting, causing sorrow and pain.
So I'm begging you now, come and make a house call.
I need you here to unclog my love drain.

Okay, not the greatest lyrics in the world, but I just wanted to type everything out the way I would do a song in a show. I didn't go back to fix things or make it better, and I think I could sell that little set of lyrics.

A Course on the Chorus

I've already told you to keep things simple and to use few words, but that really comes into play with the chorus. The chorus can be your go-to part of the song if you don't make it too difficult. I like to use two or three words and just repeat them. In the plumbing love song example above, I would be very likely to repeat something like this for the chorus:

Be my plumber of love.
My plumber of love.
You're sent from above,
My plumber of love.

Keeping the chorus simple and easy creates something that is hard to mess up, and it frees you up to think about the next verse. It takes a little practice, but you'll soon find it easier and easier. A simple chorus also works well for doing duets, but I'll talk about that in a moment.

Putting It All Together

You have all the elements you need to put together your song's lyrics; now you just need the music. It helps if you know a little bit about music theory and have a good ear. If you don't, I really can't teach you that in a book, so you're on your own there, but perhaps the person playing your music can help you.

I use the simplistic approach here as well. Slow songs will give actors a chance to sing and think, and that's good for everyone. I would also suggest keeping things centered around a few notes. You don't need a lot of runs to impress an audience.

But do pay attention to the mood of the song. While I say that it's best to use few words and sing slowly, that doesn't always work if the music you're singing to is fast and bouncy. You'll need to match the style of your singing to that music. It's like getting into character.

And don't be afraid to take a moment and just do a little "emoting acting" before a verse. This will give you time to think while your accompanist plays a little something. It also will help set the mood of the piece. If you act through this, you can make it look like it's all a part of the song and not just you taking a breather to think.

Duets

If two actors perform a duet well, it's always going to get an ovation from the crowd. Duets can be scary to do, but they also can be very simple.

First, it's very important to listen to each other. That's true in any improv, but more so here. The first singer should do a verse or two before hitting the chorus. Here it is very important to keep the chorus simple. Then the second singer sings her verse (the same number of verses as the first singer) and sings the exact same chorus.

Now comes the magic. Both singers will now repeat what they've just done, at the same time. It will end with them singing the chorus together. If your singers know what they're doing, they can harmonize on the chorus. They should know in advance who is going to take harmony, but if in doubt, have both do melody. To the audience it will sound like something from a Broadway musical, and they will respond with rowdy applause.

Long-Form Improv

Short- and long-form are the two main styles of improv. Let's talk about the difference between them, and then I will let you in on a little secret (the last part might get me a few enemies).

Short-form improv is basically what you see on TV. A few actors take a suggestion from the crowd and a set of rules from a "game," and then play it out. They often go for laughs and hopefully hit a big ending so that they can end the scene on a high point.

Long form is thought of as a more story- and character-based performance where the actors and audience can become more invested in what is happening. The enjoyment for the audience comes from the connections and the layers that the characters and plots bring.

I like both styles. I've done them both for many years, though much more in the short-form realm. But the reason I like them both is because (and here's the secret) they both follow the same rules to be successful.

If I could say what really makes them different, I'd say that short-form is more for the audience and long form is more for the actors. This is why you see several short-form but no long-form TV shows. And that's why you'll find short-form troupes playing every weekend. It's also why actors will say that long-form is the best and "purest." Another way I describe it is to say short-form players are entertainers first who often create art, and long-form players are artists first who often entertain.

But basically anything you need to do in one form holds true in the other. You have to craft a scene, you have to work and trust as a team, and you need to be in the scene at all times and go with the flow. Essentially, no matter which form you choose, you still have to do improv.

Keeping Scenes Moving

Long-form improv doesn't have the set ending that most short-form games have. It's up to you and the team to keep things moving. This is where long-form can become that crazy mix of fear and excitement that we all love so much. But don't think that it is the "lawless Wild West" of improv. As I've mentioned, you have to do all the things we've talked about for short-form improv, and you will also find that long-form also has "games" of its own—though most players don't like to call them "games." You'll find a few listed in the book and even more online, and they have their own set of how-to-play guidelines.

But one thing is for sure: You have to keep moving in long-form. You're not going to get bailed out by an emcee calling the end of a game or be able to come up with a big laugh that will take things to a nice conclusion. You are in for a wild ride, one that will allow you to build characters and scenes like never before.

Swiping a Scene

While short-form games usually have a rigid form to produce the ending of a scene, long-form games often involve several scenes in a row. The best way to go from one scene to the next is called a "swipe." The actors who will perform the next scene will simply walk in front of the scene currently going on and begin the new scene.

With a swipe of a scene, the actors from the previous scene move off stage quickly and without saying anything further. It's like a film edit in which one scene moves on to the other. Those making the swipe should focus on just the right moment to come in. Pay attention to what is happening on stage. Subtle clues from the actors will tell you whether they are building up to something more, or if they are just waiting for the scene to close. Don't push your way on stage in the middle of someone's line; come in on the normal break.

Another thing is that the actors coming on stage should be at the ready. You can tell if someone wants to come on stage; the actors already there will feel it and try to wrap up what they are doing.

Swiping will take some practice to get right, but in the hands of actors who know what they're doing, it can be seamless and take on a filmlike quality. This is when magic starts to happen in long-form.

Bear in mind that in some games, the swipe will not only move from one connecting scene to another, but it will also signify the complete end of one thought process and a move to a completely unrelated scene. It depends on the form you choose. Also, a swipe can come from people within the current scene. Two-member troupes doing the long-form will have to call an end to their own scene to start the next one. When this happens, it helps if the actor making the change in scene makes a total character change. This not only lets the audience know that something different is coming, but more importantly it alerts the teammate to the change.

An alternative to the swipe comes when the actors on stage call their own scene and make an exit. This obviously works well, but it's good to clue-in your troupe-mates that this is coming. You want the off-stage players to know that your scene is about to end so that they can come on. If you catch them with nothing planned, it will be obvious to the audience and disjoint the flow. It may also make the other actors look "clueless," and that could make them trust you less.

Working Within a Theme

One aspect of long-form that I enjoy is that you can explore many elements of the same theme. In fact, a theme is usually all you'll have to go on when starting. This gives you a chance to look at your theme from all sides, and this can lead to wonderful, unexpected things on stage. To make this happen, you have to rely on the rest of your team. They need to be ready for anything that comes up, and so do you.

I like to really look at the theme and explore it from every angle, and what's great about doing it in a long-form setting is that there will usually be a few different scenes based on that theme. That means that if you come up with something off the wall, it won't mess things up because at least one of the other scenes will be more straightforward within that theme.

When I think of how one theme can mean different things to different people, I often refer to my favorite movie, *Love, Actually.* The theme of the movie is obviously love, but take a look at all the ways the movie examines it. We have family love, new love, love of a friend, hidden love, broken love, love of one's job, and many others. I like to think of that movie as the world's greatest long-form based on one theme, and it examines every nook and cranny of that theme.

Be Ready to Explore

Long-form will give you the chance to explore many aspects of improv that short-form will limit. One of these is character. In long-form, you will have more time to work through your character, and, depending on the game that you choose, you may be able to grow that character through a series of scenes. I especially love this ability to expand when doing things like a fully improvised play or musical. The chance to use one scene to introduce a character and then come back to him a few more times to add layers is wonderful. And the best part is those "layers" can be added based on information that is coming from the other scenes and actors.

Earlier I talked about CROW (the acronym for important improv scene details such as **c**haracter, **r**elationship, **o**bjective, and **w**here; see page 9). In a short-form, you decide on answers to those four areas, and you use them to complete the scene. But in long-form, you can have some of those elements change. More than likely your character will stay the same, but the relationships, objectives, and even the where can change throughout the course of the form.

Closing Thought

Over the course of my improv life, I've run into many people who say that one form of improv—either short or long—is better than the other. The argument goes that if you don't like one form, it's because you can't do it. But as I've pointed out, both require the same elements to be successful, and both have their elements of reward. Play both. Explore both. Enjoy improv.

Performing a Show

Now that you have the basics under your belt, you might as well show what you've learned and get an audience. In putting that together, you're going to want to have a few things figured out.

The Troupe

Having the right people in your troupe is key. We've talked about the teamwork aspect of improv many times, but you also want to make sure that your troupe is supported by a solid foundation of friendship, respect, and balance.

It's important that the troupe gels. I like to make sure that the people on my stage are people who I would also hang out with off stage. It just makes sense. You're comfortable joking around with your friends, and it should be that same way on stage.

Our troupe, Quick Wits

Avoid having people play who will disrupt that group feeling. It doesn't matter how talented a player is; if he is poison backstage (meaning he brings negative energy), it's going to hurt the troupe. You're far better off with going with a group mentality than relying on certain people being stars.

The second quality to look for is balance within the troupe. A troupe includes different types of players (physical, character, wordsmith, setup, musical, audience charming, etc.), and you'll want to have players that can fill some or all of those slots. Of course, many actors will fill more than one slot, and you'll find a few who can do pretty much everything, but the main thing is to make sure that you're balanced. If you can't make that happen, be sure to choose the games that best suit the players you have.

Choose Your Style

We talked about long-form and short-form as being the two main styles for improv, and you're going to want to pick one of them to be your troupe's backbone. I wouldn't suggest trying to do both in a show. It confuses the crowd: People who came to see the short-form will wonder what's going on when you switch things up. I have done shows where we used short-form as a 30-minute warm-up before doing a 30-minute play and then an hour-long musical. That seemed to work a little as we gradually moved things up, but still, I'd generally stick with one style.

You will also need to determine what type of troupe you have in terms of how you will perform. One thing that sets our Quick Wits shows apart from many other troupes is the banter that takes place on stage between the games. That is our style. We play everything big and take a lot of chances, but that doesn't have to be your style. The actors you have often dictate how your shows will come out. Watch that and don't try to force anything different.

Now to look at a few different styles of improv shows you can do.

Straight-Up Format

This is the format that is used most often in improv. It's also how you'll see long-form troupes perform for the most part. This style is basically bringing out your troupe and working your way through a set series of games. Actors will perform with each other throughout the show. The mix of who plays what can be random or predetermined. One might look at this as the *Whose Line Is It Anyway?* type of format.

This style is highly recommended for any troupe starting out and looking to get their footing. It's also great for small troupes since you can do this easily with only four players.

Competitive

This style is popular with troupes like ComedySportz and is how most Quick Wits shows will go. The popular method is to have two three-player teams square off against each other with one team coming out the winner.

Judging the outcome is different in many troupes. Sometimes the emcee will score points; sometimes the audience will judge. Occasionally I'll see a show that is competitive in name only; no winner is ever chosen.

I like to choose audience members at the start of the show to act as the judges. I give them cards that rank from 3 to 5 in points and then a card to represent each team. These last cards will be used in games where both teams play at the same time and the judges must decide who played the best.

The scores are usually kept close (hence the 3- to 5-point range in the score cards). This is important because I don't want one team to get too far ahead of the other. The secret about our shows is that we want them to come down to the final game. Then each team plays one last game, and the audience chooses (using applause and other noise) who gets the final ten (or more) points to be the winner.

You can find a few different scoring systems online or you can even contact me for more information on our style. Better still, find something that sets you apart and make it your own.

One-Winner Competitions

These give players from different troupes the chance to perform in the same show, battling it out until a single actor is chosen as the winner. We have developed two styles for this.

The first, "Survivor," started after the first season of the television show and is still played today. I have seen versions of this on the Internet, but our version starts with eight actors who are divided randomly into two tribes. Each team plays a game, and the audience chooses the winner. The losing team votes one of its members out (pretty cruel, I know). This continues for a few rounds until you have five actors left. Then we play a "step-out" or "team" game (any game where all actors are on stage together) in which the audience members pick their favorite player, and that person gets immunity. The actors then vote another person off the stage, and you're down to four.

In the second round, the four remaining players are put into two teams and play a game. This time, the winning team chooses one of the losing team members to go. Then we have all five of the players who were kicked off play a game, the winner of which gets back in. Now back to four players, we again randomize the actors, play a round, and get back to three players. We then play another step-out game, the winner gets to cut another player, and we're down to the final two.

For the final round, the two remaining actors pick from the cast-off players to form a team for the final battle. Each team plays their game, the audience decides the winner, and the captain of that team is the sole survivor.

The Battle Royale

The One-Winner Competition is a fun but cutthroat style of play. But one drawback is that sometimes players will come out to play and get knocked off early. To address this, we came up with the Battle Royale.

Using nine players, the Battle Royale begins round one by randomizing players into three three-person teams. Each team will play a game and be scored by an independent judge who will give the game between twelve and fifteen points. Then each of the three actors is brought to the front, and the audience picks an MVP for that game. This actor receives one bonus point.

After round one, we do a step-out game, and the judge picks the three best lines for that game, giving the actors one point each.

For the next round, we randomize the teams again, and this time the actors not in the scene choose a game for the remaining team to play. The scoring continues as before. One more step-out game and the first half is over.

The second half opens much like the first, but this time we let the audience choose the games that our three-person teams play.

In the final round, the teams are randomized and play a game, but we don't choose an individual MVP. Instead we let the audience pick the game they liked the best, and that team gets an extra two points for each team member. Scores are tallied and a winner is chosen.

One key here is that the actors and audience never know the score until we know the winner. We will call out the three top scorers and then announce a winner, but the final scores aren't known. The hidden part of this is that the MVP points awarded by the audience are the key to victory. In the end, the audience has decided the winner, and we've never had a game where the winner didn't get the two points at the end.

What's great about this format is that no one ever has to leave the stage. You also never know whom you're going to be playing with until the teams are drawn. This allows you to play with different people and styles. You also don't know what games you're going to play for much of it until the game is given to you.

The Emcee

The emcee is an often-undervalued part of a short-form show. The emcee is often like an on-stage coach. She will have to pick up on what the audience is enjoying in terms of both styles and players and try to feed that to them for the rest of the show. Every game will depend on her because she will be fielding audience suggestions, calling the end to the games, etc. I'm often more worn out at the end of shows I emcee than those in which I'm just a player.

First of all, the emcee needs to be strong and have control over the audience. When the emcee speaks, everything else needs to stop. If you're the emcee, make sure that you take the stage front and center and speak clearly and with purpose. Use the beginning of the show to fire up the crowd and get everyone excited. You're the ringmaster of this circus.

When describing a game, do it quickly and clearly. I've played some games for close to 20 years, and I've described them the same way all of those years. I've got it down to where I can give the descriptions without putting a lot of thought into them, which is good because I'm usually still reading the crowd.

Getting a suggestion is also key. I listen to what the crowd is saying and give some thought to what I might do with a suggestion like that. I won't take a suggestion I don't think the players will have a few ways to play; I'm looking out for the actors. I will also make sure that the suggestions I'm taking will keep the show going in a style the audience appears to enjoy. You can usually tell quickly what the crowd prefers, and it's best to feed that.

As the game is going, keep an eye not just on the scene but also on the audience. See what they're reacting positively to and what they're not. They will guide you and help you through a good show.

Ending a game is a crapshoot sometimes. Often the actors will think that you've ended too early or let the scene go too long, but just do your best. Remember that it's always better to end quickly on a big laugh than it is to let the scene go too long. A high point is always a good place to end. At times actors will tell you that they were about to drop an even bigger laugh, but just be glad that you got out with the laugh you got.

When you do end a game, make sure you do it strong. Come front and center on the stage again and make your announcement with force. You can say various things to end a game. I like to call it by adding the name of the game or team somewhere in the close, but you can do what comes naturally. Just make sure that you take control.

After you've ended, there will likely be some applause and maybe some banter from the actors. Let the applause go until it is just starting to die down before moving on. The banter is a little trickier because you don't know where it's going to go. But make sure not to let it take over the show. You are in control.

Mix Everything Together and Enjoy

That's about it. You have your troupe, and you know what you're going to do; now just go out there and do it. You'll find that some of the things you are doing work well and some don't. Just keep cutting the parts that aren't working and keep the rest. The show I do now is nowhere near what it was when I started. And it changes whenever a new group of players come into the mix.

Never stop trying to learn more about the craft. See improv whenever you can and try to play with different troupes. I've been doing this almost every weekend for nearly 20 years. I can't even imagine how many shows I've done over the years, but I can tell you one thing—I always look forward to the next one.

Improv Off the Stage

The rules of improv work very well in everyday life. Improv teaches you to look at ways around saying "No" and finding a solution that works for both sides. It teaches you about teamwork and about doing more watching and listening than talking. And best of all, it teaches you that your opinions matter and that with the right support group you can try anything you want and someone will have your back.

Sure, that sounds a little Pollyannaish, but wouldn't it be great if life were like that? And it's not so far-fetched. The more I treat people in real life the way I treat them on stage, the more I find that they'll do the same in return...even when they don't know they're doing it.

With improv as a background, I find that I'm a better problem solver, a quicker decision maker, and more of a team player. I have more patience with others, and I don't get upset as much. These abilities have served me well throughout the years.

The point is, it doesn't matter what you do in your "real life." It will be much better and more rewarding with the confidence and understanding of teamwork that you find in improv.

About the Games
in This Book

The following games are just a sampling of games that I play with my troupe and in classrooms everywhere. I tried to give you different types of games so that you can work to make your troupe well rounded. The games given here, along with those found in the first book, should be enough to put together a very cool show.

Find your favorites and work through them, discovering all the little nuances that will make them even better. Also try out the games that you think you won't like. You might be very surprised. It's amazing how many games we play on a regular basis that started off as games no one wanted to try.

I've also tried to give you a little more than just a list of games and brief descriptions. You'll see a section for the emcee/teacher so you'll know what to look for in the game as well as a section for the actors. In most cases, I've also added some keys to success for the game. This should help you in discovering how to make games better through workshops.

Key to the Icons Used in the Games

To help you find games suitable for a particular situation, all the games are coded with symbols or icons. These icons tell you at a glance some things about the game:

- the level of difficulty—beginner, intermediate, or advanced
- the size of group needed—any size, pairs, small group (three to five), or large group (five and up)
- if props are required
- if music is required

These icons are explained in more detail below.

You can work all of the games to be different from what the icons indicate, but the icons will give you an idea of where to start. The "Team vs. Team" and "Line-Up" games are all set for more than five performers but can be practiced with fewer. Likewise, you might find games listed as "Advanced" that you consider very easy. It all depends on your level of ability.

Two icons included in other SmartFun books—age level and time—have been omitted here. All of these games take about five minutes to play, and they can be played over and over again to give every player a turn. And we have not included age levels for these games because every game in this book can be (and has been) played by children as young as nine. Adults and teens might play a game better than children, but no one could play a game with more enthusiasm.

Level of difficulty. These categories reflect the lowest level of experience necessary for players to enjoy the game. But even advanced players may learn a great deal and have a great deal of fun playing some of the "beginner" games.

 = The game is suitable for beginners.

 = The game is suitable for intermediate to advanced players.

 = The game is for advanced players only.

Number of players. Most of the games are best played by a small group of two to four players. Games that are suitable for large groups will be marked as such.

 = The actors play individually.

 = The actors play individually, and any size group can play.

 = The actors play in pairs.

 = The actors play in a small group of three to five.

 = The actors play together in a large group of five or more.

Whether you need props. Most of the games require no special props. In some cases, props, audiovisual equipment, or other materials will enhance the game. These games are flagged with the following icon, and the necessary materials are listed under the Props heading.

 = Props are needed.

Music is required. Only a few games in this book require recorded music. If the music is optional, it is noted as such; if it is required, the icon below is used:

 = Music is required.

The Games

Warm-Up Games

Warm-ups are a good way to get your mind thinking quickly. Some are designed just to get you laughing and making a lot of noise. When you want to do good improv, it's best to get the blood pumping before you start.

Run through some of these each time you get together to workshop. Some people will look at these as a waste of time at the beginning, but keep pushing it. Your actors will grow to love priming the improv pump.

In all honesty, my troupe doesn't warm up in a traditional fashion. I use these games in training classes, but before a Quick Wits show, we're more likely to just goof around with each other and laugh a lot. Then we just take that attitude on stage and run with it. A good warm up is whatever gets your mind ready to perform.

1 Devo

For the emcee/teacher: Gather the actors in a circle. Choose one actor to start. Have him turn to the actor to his left and make a movement and a noise. The second actor then turns to the actor to her left and makes the exact same

movement and noise. This continues around the circle as far as you'd like before you start with a new person and noise.

This game teaches the "watch and listen" principle of improv. Instruct the actors to copy the noise and action of the actor to their right, not that of the person who started it.

For the players: Your only goal is to match the action and sound given to you. If the actor next to you laughs, coughs, or whatever, you need to do the same. Do not correct anything; just repeat what was done before you. The game is called "Devo," which is short for de-evolution, and that is what will happen to your original noise and action if the actors are playing it correctly.

Variation Have two actors do a scene and then have two different actors repeat it as closely as they can. Then bring in two more actors and so on. You can have new actors do this as many times as you want, but, in the end, the first two actors should now get a chance to do it again.

2 Five Things

For the emcee/teacher: This game is played in a circle. One person turns to another and gives him a topic, such as "dogs." The chosen person must now come up with five things within that category. Once he does this, he will turn to the next person and give her a topic.

The idea is to practice creating lists. This is a great improv skill, especially for musical games. It also allows you to look for things outside of the typical, everyday items that come to mind.

For the players: Don't be afraid to say the first five things that come to mind. That's the real exercise here; trust your instincts. You might not give five perfect things, but it will show where your mind went when you were given the suggestion.

For instance, given the topic "dogs," you might list breeds of dogs. But you might also say, "hot" or "corn," and those also are types of dogs. In improv, go with your first instinct—then make it work.

3 Chinese Proverb

For the emcee/teacher: This game is about writing a Chinese proverb. One actor starts the "writing" by saying one word. Each actor adds another word, and this continues until the group feels that the proverb is complete. Think of this proverb as something you might find in a fortune cookie.

A group mind-set is what is being practiced here. So the game has no exact end; it can end after two words if the group calls it. It's best when the group members feel it and call it themselves.

When one proverb is finished, the next actor starts another one.

For the players: Pay attention to what is being said. Work to have proverbs make sense, but don't forget that they sometimes offer strange truths. Work toward that feeling of "oneness" with the troupe.

4 Barney

For the emcee/teacher: An actor is given a letter of the alphabet. She then comes up with a name, object, and location beginning with that letter and quickly puts them into a sentence.

If the letter is B, the actor might say, "Barney buys baseballs in Baltimore." The object of the game is to practice quick thinking.

For the players: Go with the first words that come to mind. Don't worry about making a great sentence; focus on getting your three words out quickly. This game is teaching you to spring into action.

Variation Give two actors the same letter and have them alternate sentences using that letter. The only rule: Players can't repeat any of each other's three main words, but they can repeat other words (like saying, "Barney bought bagels" and, "Barry bought bicycles"). Play until one actor can't continue.

5 Ninja

For the emcee/teacher: This is a warm-up favorite. Actors stand in a circle, each striking a Ninja pose. One actor starts, making an attack on the actor to her left. This involves making a single slicing motion toward the opponent's hand. The opponent can make one move in defense. If the attacker hits the opponent from the elbow down, she wins; the opponent then puts that arm behind his back, and it is out of play.

When an actor "loses" both arms, he is out. Play continues until there is a winner.

Once a move is made, actors must freeze until it is their turn to attack or defend again.

This game teaches body position and spatial awareness. Actors also learn control in stage combat, which occasionally occurs in improv, and having control in both attacking and defending is key.

For the players: Have fun with this but don't go crazy. You only need to tap an opponent to win, so resist the temptation to hit hard. Feel free to make noise—such as "swooshing" effects or "Hiyah!" yells—with your moves.

Variations

- This game is especially fun played in slow motion.
- Another variation is to allow players to attack to either side of them.

6 Samurai

For the emcee/teacher: This noisy game gets everyone's blood flowing. Just warn others in the area before starting to play.

Standing in a circle, each actor puts her hands together as if holding a sword. The first actor makes a downward slashing motion with her clasped hands and points to another actor. This is accompanied by a loud yell.

The targeted actor throws up his hands (still clasped) and cries out in agony. The actors to either side of the targeted actor swing their hands into his midsection (without actually touching him), also yelling.

The targeted actor then slumps over the secondary attackers and, in doing so, targets a new actor as the first did. This continues until you stop, get tired, or get asked to quiet down by others in the vicinity.

The game shows the importance of always watching a scene; you don't know when you'll be called into play. It also lets actors practice going all out in a scene. As is true of most improv, the more noise and action you give, the more fun you'll have.

For the players: Don't hold back. Make it look as if you're putting everything into your swing. When you're hit, look and sound like a wounded warrior. This is one of the games that makes actors laugh the most and is requested often as a warm-up.

Variations

- Break up the swordplay by having actors experiment with other attacks: casting spells, throwing fireballs, and shooting lightning from their hands.

- Call out your attack as part of your opening yell. For example, you might yell, "Lightning attack!" as you target an actor. The targeted actor yells as if she's been hit, responding appropriately to whatever was sent.

7   Shootout

For the emcee/teacher: The actors stand in a circle with their hands at their sides as if ready for a gunfight. Call out one actor's name. Immediately that actor drops to the ground dodging as the two actors at his side "fire" on him. If the actor doesn't get down quickly enough, he is shot and must act out his death. If he does get down in time, the actor who fired last is now shot and must act accordingly. Whoever gets shot calls out a name to start the game again.

This game shows actors that it's not always about winning; mostly it's about having fun.

For the players: If you're shot, go with it. There is no prize for staying alive, and it's actually more fun to act out being hit. Be a team player; take the bullet if it hits you.

If the two actors on the side aren't sure who fired first, they should both go down. Don't take the time to argue over who shot first; go with instinct on this and make your deaths glorious!

Variations

- Call out two actors' names and have those two draw on each other, with the slower one going down. The actors' names must be said quickly together.

- Have one actor just decide on a target, say that person's name, and shoot. If the target person drops in time, she can shoot at her attacker from the ground, taking him out.

8   Yes, Let's!

For the emcee/teacher: With actors in a circle, the game starts with one actor saying, "Let's…" completing the sentence with an action: "Let's slay a dragon," "Let's go to the amusement park," "Let's explore outer space." After the opening line, everyone enthusiastically responds, "Yes, let's!"

A second person speaks, adding a next step that continues the journey. For example, if we use "Let's explore outer space," a next step might be, "And let's get into our invisible rocket that gives us a full view of everything," but not, "But first let's take a shower." It's subtle, but one sentence propels the scene while the other diverts the agreed-upon action.

After every added sentence, the group responds, "Yes, let's!" The game continues until everyone feels as if they've told a good story. Sometimes it ends when an actor proclaims that they can now rest from their adventure.

This game teaches actors to wait for their turn and add something in a positive manner. Plus it's always great to play a game in which no matter what you say, everyone will agree with you loudly and happily.

For the players: It is important not to interrupt once another actor starts talking. No matter how great your sentence was going to be, you need to let the first actor speak. You will get your chance later.

Also, listen closely to the story so that your addition makes perfect sense. This doesn't mean that you can't throw in crazy ideas, but it does mean your idea should contribute to the story's logical flow.

9   Alliteration

Prop A ball or similar object that can be passed around

For the emcee/teacher: Gather your actors in a circle. Have a small ball for them to pass around. Begin by tossing the ball to an actor and announcing a letter. That actor passes the ball to the right, and each actor will do the same until it has gone around the circle.

At the same time, the actor to the left of the person who catches the ball begins saying as many words as she can that start with the letter before the ball makes it back to her. See who can come up with the most words. Leave out difficult letters such as X and Q.

This game teaches the actors to think under pressure. The reason for the ball is that it increases the pressure as the speaker sees it getting closer. This game will teach them to clear their mind and just speak words as they come to them.

For the players: Shut everything out and come up with as many words as you can. Speak clearly and don't try to go too fast because it will mess you up.

If you're passing the ball around, try to move it quickly. To do this, you have to keep an eye on its progress. This is always a good improv skill to practice.

Variation In a small group, use a stopwatch to time people and see how many words they can list in 30 seconds.

10 Say It!

For the emcee/teacher: Have two actors face each other, count "3, 2, 1," and then both say a word. This can be any word. Players then try to think of a common ground word and say that after counting down. They keep doing this until they are able to say the same word at the same time.

This game emphasizes cooperation, teaching your actors to think as a team. Credit for this game goes to Jake Suazo with the "Thrillionaires."

For the players: Clear your mind and connect with your partner. It may take a few rounds to say the same word.

Also, don't get upset if your partner doesn't say what you think is obvious. We had two actors start with "computer" and "cat." To many, the next word might be "mouse," and you'd have the very rare first-round win, but while one actor said "mouse" the other said "keyboard." It took us a moment to realize that he meant the viral video of "keyboard cat" and his answer made sense. They both said "computer" on the next turn, and all was forgiven.

Variation Although this game gets hard with more than three people, I recommend trying a third person, but be ready for longer games.

Single-Player Games

Occasionally there is a need for a game that one person can play. This can be part of a show, a warm-up exercise, or an audition. Here are a few games to try out.

I don't push a lot of solo improv because there isn't much of the team aspect to it, but you'll find that these games can be turned into team games with just a few tweaks. Also, although these games will be labeled "beginner" games, an experienced actor can take these simple games and turn them into great scenes.

11 No, You Didn't

For the emcee/teacher: One actor begins telling a story based on a topic you name. He goes along until you interrupt, saying something like, "No, you didn't" or whatever fits with what he has said. The actor will then respond, "You're right," and change the story.

Your job is to find the right moments to make the actor change the story. You want to hit pivotal moments. Perhaps he's declared: "I was climbing up the ladder." You interrupt: "No, you weren't." And the actor responds: "You're right; I was using my hover boots."

Don't overdo it. Interrupt only here and there so that the story stays interesting.

This game will help players think quickly.

For the players: Be ready to change quickly. The idea to the game is that you were caught in a lie and now have to give the "truth." It needs to come quickly and honestly, no matter how strange it might be.

Begin with a simple story. Build the strangeness slowly; this will give you a better chance to keep things flowing. As in real life, the more big lies you tell, the harder it is to keep them straight.

Variation Try this game with two people. In this instance, the two people tell the story until one is "caught in the lie." Then the other picks up the story and keeps it going until they get called out again.

12   What Happens Next?

For the emcee/teacher: This game doesn't need an emcee, so you can play completely by yourself. An actor asks the audience what they want acted out. The actor starts the scene, and when they reach a point where a choice might be made or an event might take place, the actor freezes and asks the audience, "What happens next?" They then act out whatever the audience tells them to do. This continues until you come to the next logical stopping point.

For the players: Most of what you need to do is spelled out above. Make sure that you are creating your world here. The more you see it, the more the audience will see, and since they are the ones putting strange things into it, they want to see them. That means you HAVE to see them.

Variation This can be done with a group of actors going and even an emcee who can call "Freeze" to stop the scene before asking the audience, "What happens next?"

13   Sybil

For the emcee/teacher: In this game an actor will tell a story, but that story will change once different characters and situations are called out. These changes will affect the story and carry through the scene.

As in most games where an emcee is calling changes, it's best to go from one extreme to the other. For instance, if you have the actors being "happy," switch to "sad" or "mad" as opposed to switching to "love." Contrasting mood swings will create the most fun. The same is true of switching characters.

Stick to changing one element—either all emotions or all characters. Otherwise the game can get tricky. For instance, if the actors are being sad, and you call out "pirate," should they be sad pirates, or should they leave the sad part behind and just be pirates? Either way is fine, but they'll need to know what you expect before doing the scene.

For the players: Be ready to change at any time. Have a mind-set of "How is this new emotion or character affecting me?" and you'll need to answer that quickly. If you are happy and suddenly you are asked to be mad, figure out what is happening at this second to make you mad.

Keep the story going in a very logical manner. It all needs to fit like puzzle pieces so that it stays true to its beginning and has the scene elements that we've discussed.

Variations

- Actors can play this game as a scene. The game "Emotions" (a variation on Game #76, "Accents") shows you exactly how this variation works.

- I've also played this as a game for kids. They give me a book to read, and I start reading, but after a little bit I'll stop and ask them to give me an emotion. I then continue reading in that emotion. I've also reread the same paragraph in different emotions to show them how their emotions can change everything.

14 ACE

For the emcee/teacher: The three letters in ACE stand for *action, color,* and *emotion.* In this story-telling game, the emcee dictates *how* the actors will tell a story—The emcee starts by calling out one of these three words, and the actors must focus on and describe only that aspect (for example, the emotion of the event). When the emcee calls out one of the other two words (for example, action), the actors must continue with the same story but switch to talking about the actions involved in the story.

Think of it this way: *Action* is what the character is doing. *Emotion* is what he feels. For this game, *color* means the environment in which the story takes place; what the character sees.

This game encourages actors to focus on one area of a story.

For the players: It's challenging to keep the story going when the emcee's calls keep switching among the three ACE focuses. One moment you're talking about *action* and *emotion* when suddenly *color* is called. Now you can describe only the sights and sounds.

Concentrate on the area that has been called and try telling the story in both first- and third-person.

Variation Try a three-person version of this game, assigning each person one of the three story focuses. The emcee points to an actor (action, color, or emotion) to begin the story and jumps to another to hear the story continue from another point of view.

Basic Games

These games are the backbone of improv. That doesn't mean that they're easy games; it means that they have a little bit of everything in them. You can use games like these with any style of troupe and come out with strong performances.

You can also use these games in rehearsals to work on areas you want to see improved. For instance, you might have a troupe that likes to play a game like "Overactors Anonymous" (Game #16) in a physical style. Have them play it with an emphasis on character instead and watch them respond.

This rehearsal method is great for expanding a troupe's abilities.

15 Revolver

For the emcee/teacher: This game gets several different scenes going at the same time. Four actors stand in a "square" pattern. The two "front" actors (#1 and #2) are given a scene to act out. The actors then rotate clockwise, and actors #2 and #3, now in front, are given a scene. Continue until there are four scenes total, with each actor having acted in two scenes.

The emcee starts the scene with the first two actors. When the actors feel the time is right, the emcee calls either "Clockwise" or "Counterclockwise." The actors rotate and perform the scene for that pairing. This continues, giving equal time to all scenes, until the game is called.

For the players: The scenes are going to be short so you need to come into the scene with a bang. Don't worry about setting anything up; jump right into it. For example, if your scene is about parachuting, don't start with, "Are you ready to get in the plane?" You can be in the plane or even be jumping as the scene starts.

Be ready when the scene comes back to you. It should be as if your scene had continued while you were away, and now we've cut back to see where you've taken things. The nice thing about "Revolver" is that you have time to think about where you want to go. This is good practice for doing long-form, especially a fully improvised play.

Variation Have the characters "freeze" in the revolve. This means that if you were bent over in a scene as the emcee called "Clockwise" and you're in the next scene, you'll still be bent over. Now you will have to work with that position into the new scene.

16   Overactors Anonymous

For the emcee/teacher: Given a very boring subject, the actors have to create the most exciting scene possible. To do this, they have to overact every aspect of it.

This game can be used to teach big characters, big word play (monologues), big emotions, and even big physical play. I've seen actors take a simple poke to the chest and react as if they'd been shot with a cannon. I've seen them work a math book as if it were 200 pounds and four feet wide. This game is perfect to get your actors outside their comfort zones but still have a lot of fun.

For the players: Be ready to up the stakes with every line. Keep in mind that that doesn't mean you have to be overaggressive or loud in a scene. That is not what this is about. Overacting can come in many forms.

Be ready to match your fellow actors so that the scene makes sense. If they are overacting a certain point, join them to help create the illusion that you're all as bad (or good, depending on how you're looking at it).

17   Infomercial

For the emcee/teacher: In this game, actors take an item that would be hard to sell and build an infomercial around it. Let the actors experiment with the different ways that this can be done and find what works best for them.

One angle is to have a player act as the host. He talks directly to the audience as if they are in the studio, encouraging them to respond to questions like, "Have you ever had a problem with [blank]?" or "Have you ever wished that you had a

[blank]?" Getting the crowd into the scene and making it an event will sell the scene.

The host brings on other actors as people such as "the inventor," "the doctor who can prove it works," "someone who has used the product," or any other staple of an infomercial. Find ways to get everyone excited about a product that has no excitement factor.

For the players: Look for ways to build the scene. If you're the host, pump up everything as if it's the best thing ever. If you're brought into the scene, find a character who works well for the product. Involve the audience. You can even bring them up on stage for testimonials or go into the crowd with a microphone.

Variation In the variation "Telethon," actors take something that has no business being the subject of a telethon (like NFL quarterbacks) and build a telethon around it. The host brings people on to talk about the plight of the [subject]. This ends with all the actors joining in a "We Are the World" type song that is supposed to get people to donate.

18 Movie Mad Lib

Prop A custom Mad Lib

For the emcee/teacher: For this game, you need to create a "Mad Lib" that sounds like a movie trailer. (Below is a generic one you can use, but feel free to create one that you like.)

> In a world where [plural noun] is against the law, one [occupation] took a stand against the [organization] to right a wrong. Filmed on location in [location], [famous actor] in his most challenging role will make you feel [emotion] like never before in this [movie genre] that dares to ask: [question].

Ask the audience to help you fill in the blanks, without letting them know the context. Just tell them that you need a "plural noun," an "occupation," etc. Read the finished piece back to them. The actors will then act out the trailer that goes with it.

For the players: This is a silly game, but the audience will get a kick out of you being able to work a good trailer around the craziness. Note: With this game, it is important to hit all of the mentioned details. The audience can be unforgiving when they know what is supposed to happen and details are missed.

This game encourages you to "up the ante" whenever you can. Look at ways to bring characters and physical comedy into the scene, but as snippets of the movie. Remember that most trailers are not one long scene; be prepared to break things up a bit.

Variation Open a show with "Previews of Coming Attractions." To do this, get a list of famous actors and a list of made-up movie titles from the audience before the show. Players then draw an actor's name and a movie title and create a trailer.

19 Michael Bay History

For the emcee/teacher: Act out a moment in history as if famed director Michael Bay were doing a big screen adaptation of it. It is good if your actors already know Bay's work. He's responsible for movies such as *Transformers, Pearl Harbor,* and *Armageddon.* Subtlety is not his strong point. Actors should watch at least one of his movies to get an idea of the cartoon characters and dialogue that always show up in his films.

For the players: It is fun to take a historical event and "Bay It Up." We've had the Lincoln assassination turn into a crazy scene involving aliens and dinosaurs, and we've seen the signing of the Declaration of Independence almost stopped by Redcoat robots.

But don't just work over-exhausted action into your scenes. You can also use the strange love stories or the overly heroic characters Bay uses in his films.

Variation You can also "Bay It Up" with normal scenes. This comes very close to "Overactors Anonymous" (Game #16), but it can be different if played right. Or try other directors and see what you can do.

20   Scene with a Soundtrack

Music Several selections of music from soundtracks representing different moods

For the emcee/teacher: This game involves a musical improviser who will change up the scene by playing different soundtrack music under the scene. Actors match the style of acting to the music.

Use a generic situation for this scene since the scene will get crazy enough as it progresses. The sound person should let the scene develop a little before starting into the music. Don't play the music selections too long before fading out. Also mix up the soundtrack pieces so that you don't have songs of a similar mood back to back. The sound person can control the scene with the right choices.

For the players: Be ready for the changes and then go with it. Take a moment when you hear the song starting up to feel the mood of it. This will also give the audience a chance to hear and feel the music. Know that it's likely only going to play for 30 seconds at the very most, so hit the theme quick.

If the music is sad, think about why you would be sad in this scene right now. The same goes for any emotions that the music can create. Don't change the scene completely; stay with it but add the emotion the music is dictating.

21   A to Z

For the emcee/teacher: In this game, actors do a scene that starts with the first person using the letter *A* as the first letter of the first word he says in a sentence. The second person then uses the letter *B* as the first letter of the first word she says in her sentence, and so on until you end with an actor using the letter *Z* at the beginning of a sentence.

Actors can talk as long as they need and are usually stopped by the next actor jumping in. It's interesting to know that this scene will be exactly 26 one-line exchanges long. This will help train the actors to work a scene from introduction, to conflict, to resolution quickly. It's also easy on the emcee because the game has a built-in ending.

For the players: The biggest rule here is, "Do not mess up the alphabet." The audience will know instantly. Always be ready with the next letter. And remember that your scene has a definite ending. By the time you hit *W*, you should be near your exit. Don't overshoot it and leave a scene unresolved.

Also, don't mess up your fellow actors by throwing in your word(s) too quickly and over the top of what they are saying. Work as a team and make the scene look like a script written by an author playing a clever game.

Variations

- Have the actors act out a Shakespearean-style scene under the guidelines of "A to Z."

- Change up the alphabet. Start with any letter and work your way through the alphabet and back to it (G to G for example). This way, you don't have to end your scene on *Z* every time. You can also start with *Z* and work backward. This variation will test your actors.

Character Games

Most games can be called "Character Games," but these work specifically on character structure. Some of these are "workshop" games more than performance games. Since you'll always find plenty of performance games, having a few games to use in rehearsals to flesh things out is a good thing.

When putting together a character, you want to find details that make him or her unique. Stereotypes will work in a pinch, but adding a little bit extra will help you create something special. As an example, have your character limp. It's a simple detail, but it is one that other characters will ask about it. If you have a quick backstory about it ("Oh, that...I fended off an alien invasion in the nineties. No big deal."), your character will be much more interesting. Even if no one asks you about it, you're okay; the audience will see the character has depth.

Be careful about reusing characters too much. Some people bring out a character night after night and always give the same catch phrase. It might get laughs, but over time taking this easy way out will affect your creativity. So if you do bring out a character you've done before, give the audience some more depth each time.

22 Acronyms

For the emcee/teacher: In this game, the actors come on stage in character. It's good if each character has some sort of occupation or area of expertise. The emcee interviews them briefly so the audience will get to know each and then asks the audience for an acronym—something very common, such as SCUBA. The emcee notes that in most circles, SCUBA stands for "self-contained underwater breathing apparatus." He then asks each character what that acronym means to him.

The characters respond, coming up with something fitting their character. For instance, if the character was a pacifist pirate, he might answer that the acronym stands for "store cannons under ballast areas." While on its own that might not make sense, the character explains it a little more. The pirate, for example, might say that since he doesn't like to fight, he finds it best to hide the cannons when his crew comes upon another ship, and that is why they yell "SCUBA" to each other.

Each character will get a chance to answer. This game helps actors work within a character and also tests their ability to string words together.

For the players: Come up with a character who has "character." Since you won't act out a scene using this person—you only have to be interviewed—be as creative as possible. Just give your character an area of expertise, and it's best if it's something a little odd. The pacifist pirate is a good example.

Begin crafting your answer the second you hear the acronym. Think about the letters and how they work with your character. You'll have a little bit of time because the emcee will give its common world meaning.

Your answers will come that quickly if you remember to think character first and go for the letter that has a word that fits. And always dump something if it's not clicking into place quickly; there's usually a reason for that.

23 Character Motivation

For the emcee/teacher: Secretly give each character a motivation (for example, money, love, revenge, etc.) for this scene. Explain that the characters are not allowed to directly tell one another what it is they want; instead they must finagle what they want out of the others. Then give the group a location for a scene (a bus stop, for instance) and watch as the actors try to work each other to get what they want.

The game teaches actors how to use motivation in character development. Often when asked to do a character, an actor puts on a wig or some clothing and uses a silly voice, but it doesn't have to be like that. A driving motivation can be just as powerful in creating a character as any makeup, accent, or wardrobe.

For the players: If you take the game to heart, you can learn how to manipulate someone without your "mark" being aware of what is going on. If your motivation is "money," it is easy to keep talking about needing more cash. Instead, look for other ways to get what you want.

We often play that the actor who satisfies his motivation first is the winner. You lose if the other actors feel you were too obvious.

24 Family Dinner

For the emcee/teacher: Give each actor a secret motivation for his or her character. Each must then act on that motivation during the course of a family dinner. It's a simple concept and is close to the game "Character Motivation," seen above, but the dinner and family relationships make the game better for the stage.

For the players: Work out what happens at this dinner: Secrets can come out, conflict may arise, etc. Explore how your character interacts with the other characters.

Variations

- One variation is to have a "mom" or "dad" character trying to figure out what's going on with the other people at the table.
- This game can be a good set up for a long-form. Simply start with the dinner and see what the actors come up with. They'll find other scenes to spin out of the dinner.

25 Opposites

For the emcee/teacher: In this game, as in the two previous games, you're going to give the actors some characteristics. But in this game the traits you give the actors need to be polar opposites. For example, perhaps one character is very brave, and the other is very afraid. To set the scene, give the characters a task to perform (like defusing a bomb). The characters will have to work together, putting differences aside, to resolve the scene.

This game teaches actors to work with a difficult suggestion. It can even have bearing on real life, prepping actors to work with other actors, some of whom may be difficult to perform with.

For the players: Without giving up your character's motivation, find a way to work with the other actors' characters. This game will push you in a "Yes, and…" sort of way.

Variations

- In a game called "Goalie," one actor is surrounded by other actors that he must face one by one. Each actor presents the goalie with a character and an opening line. The goalie must respond to each quickly and in a matching character before moving on to the next person.
- Actors can also play "Opposing Goalie," coming up with an opposite character and reaction to those presented to her.

Guessing Games

I spoke a lot about this genre of games earlier in this book. As a recap, here are the main considerations when it comes to a game that involves getting one character to guess another's given endowment.

First, remember it's a scene. The audience is not watching you play charades on stage. Work in elements that will help you create a whole scene with a beginning, middle, and end. The person doing the guessing has to help sell this idea.

Second, as the clue giver, if you can see that the person you're giving clues to has no idea what you're doing, change things up. Doing the same thing over and over is frustrating for you, the other actor, and (most importantly) the audience.

26 Soothsayer

For the emcee/teacher: This is a variation of "Late for Work" (discussed in the previous book and earlier in this one). In this game the "soothsayer" is sent out while the emcee gets a few details from the audience about the future of a second player who will be coming in for a reading. I find it best to get three details about the player's future; start with something basic and let the strangeness grow in the next two predictions.

A third actor will give nonverbal clues to the soothsayer to get the right predictions. Most often, this third actor plays the part of the assistant, although sometimes he is the "real" soothsayer helping out the figurehead boss.

Once you have the suggestions, bring in the "soothsayer," and the scene begins. The customer comes in for a reading of her future, and the assistant acts out the predictions to get the soothsayer to say them out loud. The game ends when all three predictions are named correctly.

For the players: This game has three main parts, and each player has to do his or her role correctly to make it work. The most overlooked role is that of the customer. She actually knows the correct answers and can offer verbal clues to help the soothsayer. Don't be obvious with these; you just want to keep the soothsayer on track and can do this by letting the soothsayer know that something is wrong or by nudging him toward something he's said already that was close. This player also helps create a scene since they are the only one just talking about the scene.

The customer may also catch the assistant doing his charades and force him to explain what he is doing. If you're the customer, don't do this too much; it's best to do when you know the audience is laughing about what is going on behind you.

The assistant is important because he has to give the right clues. As the assistant, you have to know when your partner is not getting it and try something else. And, of course, work to keep this a scene.

The last character is the soothsayer. Go big with this character. Think of all the palm readers/mediums you've seen acted out. And remember: You are not just guessing things; you are talking to a customer. It helps if you write off the

times when you're wrong as misunderstanding the signals that you're getting from "beyond." This also will let the assistant know that what he is doing is not working.

Variation This scene can be played as a séance in which you're trying to talk to the dead. You might even try to figure out which famous historical figure you're reaching.

27 Not This but That

Prop A stopwatch

For the emcee/teacher: This game is one of the few guessing games that is not a scene. One actor leaves the room while you collect audience suggestions for three basic activities: brushing your teeth, riding a bike, walking the dog, etc. Change out one aspect of the activity for something else. In the example of "brushing your teeth," change out the toothpaste for barbecue sauce. Do this with all three suggestions.

Bring the actor back in, and let the other actors get him to guess the new activities. To do this, the actor must first see the original suggestion acted out, and then see the change. The actor can't talk during the viewing but, rather, raises his hand when he thinks he has the answer. "I was brushing my teeth," he might begin, "but instead of using toothpaste, I was brushing with barbecue sauce."

This game is given a time limit (usually 90 seconds), during which the group must present all three activities to the actor, who correctly identifies them. When the actor raises his hand, time stops. The time stops with each guess. The time left is then communicated to the team before starting the next activity.

For the players: If you're giving clues, be clear in the actions you present for the basic activity. Be equally clear about what is being replaced. This is usually done by miming that item being thrown away.

We often have two actors act out the activities so that they can do things together. It's rare that guessing games have two people working together, but it seems to work well with this game.

Variations

- Have the teams compete to see who can get all three in the least amount of time. That team will get the points for the game.

- Give 3 points for each activity the team gets right, with an extra point for getting all 3 in under 90 seconds; 3 bonus points if it's under 60 seconds. If a team doesn't get an activity correct, the other team gets a chance to give the correct answer for a bonus point.

28 Marriage Counselor

For the emcee/teacher: Send two actors out (male and female in most cases) and take audience suggestions to find a problem for each person. These should be the types of problems that would mess up a marriage, but with a twist. For example, one of them spends all the family's money on "My Little Pony" dolls.

A third player will be the counselor. The counselor's job is to give verbal clues to get the couple to announce their problems, which will bring them back together.

For the players: The couple comes back on stage and needs to create dialogue to develop a scene. As part of the couple, you will be guessing blindly at "your problems" at first but try to "zero" in on them.

As the counselor, you will facilitate the scene. Begin by asking open-ended questions and then start to give actual clues. In the "My Little Pony" example, you might ask, "Why do you need so many of these?" You're not bringing up the dolls specifically, and by being vague you're letting the couple say whatever they want. Usually this leads to strange answers.

Your questions should be directed to one person. But keep in mind that while the husband might be answering blindly, the wife can be chiming in at the same time. Give the clues a little at a time. You don't need to come out strong at first; let the scene develop for a bit. You can either mix up who you are questioning, or stick with one person until he/she has it before moving on to the other.

The game ends when both problems have been guessed correctly and the couple makes up.

29 Hijacker

For the emcee/teacher: Send one actor out while you gather information from the audience. Ask for suggestions for a bizarre method of transportation or location (this will be the thing the hijacker takes over), a strange demand (what the hijacker is asking for), and a strange threat (what the hijacker will do if demands are not met).

Call the actor on stage with a few other actors to act as hostages. Another actor, playing the part of the negotiator, will try to defuse the situation. To do this, she has to get the hijacker to guess the three details. The hostages help as needed.

For the players: Follow the rules of most guessing games, and you'll be fine. Since we've all seen movies and television with this type of scene, this is a great game for scene work.

Variation Play the game competitively with the hijacker and the negotiator leading different teams, and both trying to guess the same three answers. In this variation, the hostages will be comprised of members of both teams. They can help but have to be careful about it: If a member of one team gives a clue, only the guesser from the other team can answer. This means that you want to give a clue that would be helpful to your player but not to the other team's guesser.

30 Bong. Bong. Bong.

For the emcee/teacher: Four actors stand in a line; three are turned away from the audience with their ears covered. Give a strange activity to the fourth person, who must pass it along to the nearest actor, using only pantomime and gibberish. They have a limited amount of time to do this before a loud "bong" is heard, after which they must stop.

At this point, the second actor who was receiving the clues must now pass the information to the next person until they hear a "bong." The third actor then passes information to the final player until the "bong" is heard again. At that point, the fourth actor says what the activity was supposed to be.

For the players: You have a short amount of time, so don't waste any. Make sure that your receiver understands what you're doing.

Audience Help

I love games that involve the audience. This can be bringing them up on stage, getting some props from them, or simply asking them for information. These games work in situations where you are asked to perform for a company or group. They love seeing people they know brought into the action.

For these games, it's important to find the right audience member, especially when you're bringing people up on stage. You don't want someone who will be too stiff or doesn't want to be there, but you also don't want someone who will take too big a part of the show. Avoid people who seem too eager.

At times, you'll need to work with the audience member a little to get a performance out of him. When this is the case, give him easy things to do and make your needs obvious. For example, in the game "Sound Effects" (Game #32) an audience member makes all of the scene's sound effects. Giving your recruit prompts ("Wait! Do you hear that? It's a phone ringing.") will make his part easy and boost his confidence.

31 Between the Texts

Props Two cell phones from the audience

For the emcee/teacher: Ask the audience for two cell phones for use in a scene. Announce that in this game, two actors can say only the lines that they find in the texts on the borrowed phones. A third actor makes up dialogue so that everything makes sense.

The comedy will be easy once the audience knows that people's personal texts will be read out loud. You can make most any type of scene work here.

For the players: If you're one of the players reading the texts, scroll through as much as you can before the scene starts. This will give you a feel for the type of conversations you will have at your disposal. Be sure to note lines that might lead to good answers.

You don't have to read every word in the text. Often you'll find long texts with a line or two that will work. Use those and don't worry about reading the whole thing. Sometimes you can just say a word or two. A "Yes" or "No" when you need to buy a little more time to scan texts can be helpful.

If you're the third actor, your job is to keep the scene going. To do this, you can't force strange questions on the people reading the texts. You can't be sure that what they'll find on the phones will be the right response. It will help if you pay attention to what they're giving you from the text responses. Often you can tell where the phone discussion is going, and you can use that to your advantage in the scene.

Be careful to avoid texts that are "too private." While it might seem funny, it can get uncomfortable quickly. And that will affect not just the person whose phone you're using; the whole crowd will feel it as well.

Variation We've used the texts in musical form, singing only lines that we find on the phones. You can turn this into a duet by having the two singers put the conversation between two texters to song.

32 Sound Effects

Prop An audience member

For the emcee/teacher: As actors play out a scene, an audience member will provide all of the scene's sound effects. The actors must react to every sound as if it's the perfect sound to hear at this moment.

Coach the audience member to make whatever noise she wants whenever she wants to make it. Explain that it's up to the actors to deal with her noises. Do a test run, having the actor go through a motion and inviting the audience member to supply the sound effects. Often the person won't make much noise, so the actors will guide her, saying things like, "I'm going to open this door; it sure looks creaky."

For the players: Be ready for the noises. Initially, you won't know if you've got an active or inactive audience member, so be ready for either. If you find you have a quiet person, make sure to lead him by announcing things that will have a specific noise.

When I emcee, I usually stand near the person, so I can remind him to make more noise or do it louder.

Be careful not to talk over the person's sound effects. If you do, she will think she wasn't supposed to make a noise there and will be quiet through the scene. Without the noises, this scene can go south quickly.

Variation Have one or two actors do an action without making any sound. Another actor makes all the noises into a microphone. These noises can include little grunts or bits of gibberish as if one person is talking to himself or making small talk with the other person. If the person on the mic is a seasoned player, she will direct the scene just through the sounds she makes.

33 The Newlywed Game

Props Three audience members; blank paper; markers

For the emcee/teacher: Of all the games I've created over the years, this is my personal favorite. Keep in mind that since the game is about newlywed couples, it's more for adults than for kids. The game is based on the TV show of the same name; if your actors are not familiar with it, have them watch it on YouTube. The game plays pretty much the same, with a twist.

Give three actors a "wife" from the audience and take all six people out of the theater. While they are gone, get some answers to basic questions (see below) and record them on the paper. Get three answers for each of the three questions you choose. Each couple will need to have an answer to each question. Put each couple's answer cards in a pile with the first answer on top.

Bring the couples back on stage. Ask each couple their name (each couple will have a character type—explained in the "for the players" section) and then ask the wives the first question. When they answer, the husbands show their first card, revealing the answer they "gave" earlier and will now try to explain. Having the husbands justify their strange answers is the heart of the game.

Another aspect of the game is that the questions you asked the audience while the couples were away will change when you actually play the game. Let me give you some examples of how to turn a basic question into a "Newlywed Game" question:

"Strange location" becomes "Tell me where you first met and fell in love."

"Song title" becomes "What is 'your song,' the one you danced to at your wedding?"

"Name of a candy" becomes "Your pet name for your spouse"

"A child's game" becomes "Using the title of child's game, how would you describe your spouse's kiss?"

"TV show title" becomes "What TV show title would best describe your first date?"

"Company slogan" becomes "Use a famous company slogan to describe your honeymoon."

You will go through three rounds of this before the game ends. Make sure to ask the husbands about each of their answers.

For the players: The emcee works this like a game show. Be sure to go into that mode to help sell it.

The husbands should explain the game to the audience member "wives" while they're off stage. Tell them not to worry about trying to give actual answers to the questions but, instead, to say the first thing that comes to mind.

Each couple should also come up with their character. This will help the couples be different from each other—and make the scene even funnier. As husbands, you will likely handle most of the character work but don't be afraid to ask the volunteers for input.

34 Dating Game

For the emcee/teacher: This is another game that plays like the older TV game show of the same name. If you're unfamiliar with it, catch it online.

Take an audience member out of the theater while three actors (bachelors) are given different endowments. This can be anything: a strange job, an obsession, a historical or fictitious personality, or even the persona of an inanimate object. When the audience member/"contestant" returns, she will ask the "bachelors" questions, determining which of them she would like to go with on a date.

The game really ends when the contestant figures out who these bachelors are. We coach her beforehand on how to play the game and how it should end. When she chooses, we also want her to say something about whom she didn't choose, such as, "I didn't choose bachelor #1 because I don't like clowns" (assuming that the actor was playing a clown, of course). She then says why she picked the winner, guessing at that character.

The contestant will ask some vague "date" questions like, "Where is your perfect spot to watch the sunrise?" and "If you were a tree, what tree would you be?" Again, she can be coached before the game. The actors answer her questions, in character, giving as much information as possible without totally giving away his character.

This game gives actors practice in creating a character from elements not of their choosing. It's all about emptying one's mind and refilling it with new information.

For the players: Get into your characters. You will have to answer the questions as your characters would. If you are playing a lamp, for example, what would be the perfect way to end an evening? This is the type of thinking that you'll need to do during this game.

Body language is also a good way to get your character across. This is especially true of an inanimate object.

Variation Play this game using another troupe member as the contestant. It takes the audience out of the game, but it results in some better questions and actor interactions.

35 Pop-Up Storybook

Props A few audience members

For the emcee/teacher: One actor narrates this entire scene. The narrator needs to be an advanced actor; the others in the scene can be of various degrees of experience, or even audience members.

In the game, an actor "reads" a pop-up storybook suggested by the audience. We usually ask for the name a of children's book that hasn't been written. As the actor reads the book, the other actors and audience members will create scenes from the book, posing as if they are the "pop-ups."

To play, the reader makes a big movement across the stage (stage left to stage right), miming that he is turning pages in a large book. This movement signals the actors to get into a new position. The reader then continues the story based on the positions the actors have chosen.

To add to the "pop-up book" theme, you can do various pop-up book actions like "pull tabs" or "spin a wheel." By doing this, the actors will have to do a simple action. You can play with this by moving the tab back and forth. This is a part of the game where the reader can stop reading and tell the audience, "Look! Here's a tab I can pull."

For the players: Make sure that you are giving the reader some good poses to work with. Be sure to tell this to any participants from the audience members, so that they know to go big with their freezes. Everyone also needs to pay attention to the story being crafted and strike poses that will help move it along.

As the narrator, you can also lead the other players with some simple setups. As you're getting ready to turn the next page, make sure that you've moved back to stage left. During this move, talk about the next part of the story. You might say, "Billy knew that he had to see the world. But he didn't have a lot of transportation options," or, "That's when the most unexpected thing happened." Little setups like this alert the other actors without pushing things too much.

Variations

- Do this game without the audience members.
- You can also use this type of setup for a long-form improv scene where each new scene is triggered by the turn of a page.

36 Driver's License

Props An assortment of driver's licenses from the audience

For the emcee/teacher: This game is about looking at the picture of a face and creating a character based on it. The actors use driver's licenses, submitted by the audience, recreate the person's face, and keep it through the entire scene. Is the person super happy? Tough looking? A person's face can give you much to work with in a scene.

To switch things up, we sometimes take two licenses for each actor so that they can switch characters during the scene.

For the players: Exaggerate the face and the character you create from it. You need to keep the same look of the face but give it a little extra to make the scene more fun for the audience.

Maintain that face and the character throughout—no matter what's going on in the scene. If you are using an unhappy-looking face and your character needs to be happy, figure out how to express that without breaking your character's unhappy nature. And knowing the faces and the characters that the other actors have to maintain, you can create some interesting interactions. For example, give a person with a "happy face" some bad news.

Variation Some venues, such as a school, might make driver's licenses harder to come by. To play this game without them, give audience volunteers an emotion and have them make the biggest face they can with that emotion. The actors will copy the face and hold it throughout the scene.

37 Human Prop

Prop One audience member

For the emcee/teacher: Actors perform a scene using an audience member as whatever prop or scenery they need to complete the scene.

Explain that improv almost never uses props or scenery, but that will change now because an audience volunteer has agreed to act out all of those things. As in "Sound Effects" (Game #32), you'll want to do a test run with the volunteer so he can see what to do. For example, announce that an actor needs to enter through a door and have the volunteer be the door. Act that out, and your volunteer is ready to go.

As in some other games, the actors might have to prompt the audience volunteer about the scene's needs. We often find ourselves having to mention a needed object a few times and pointing to where it's supposed to be. The volunteer usually catches on.

For the players: You may get some strange suggestions from the audience member "prop"; be ready to use what he gives you. It might help to start with some simple ideas first to ease him into the game.

We enjoy putting the volunteer into strange situations. Having someone from the audience suddenly jump on your back to play a backpack or wrap himself around you to become a winter coat are moments that will get big reactions from the audience. Be careful to avoid pushing the volunteer too far; it's bad for the person and could stop your scene.

This is one of the best games to play at a corporate event because everyone knows each other and the strange positions will bring even more laughter.

Variation You can use other troupe members as the human prop. In this version the "prop" actors can fill a lot more of a scene.

Team vs. Team Games

In this book, I wanted to present some games that are fun to use when doing a competitive style of improv. As noted earlier (see page 26), Quick Wits plays competitively in most of our stage shows, and this style is often used when two troupes want to do a show together. You don't have to make the whole show competitive, but doing a few sections of it competitively will be fun to try.

Always keep in mind that the real goal of these games is not to win; it's to entertain the audience. To do this, make sure that you're not setting up the other team or troupe for failure. You can make it tough but not impossible; that's not good for the show. And, yes, winning the game is the second goal, so go for it. After the game has been played, the emcee can then ask the audience to choose a winner.

38 Big, Bigger, Biggest

For the emcee/teacher: Divide the group into two teams. One team performs a basic scene that is then recreated by the other team, only a little bigger. The first team then repeats the scene, stepping it up even more. Finally the second team gets one more crack at the game, making it as big as possible.

For the players: To make this game work, the original scene must have basic elements that can be built up. This can include things discussed (for example, what characters see in the distance) and actions taken (characters look at the

object through binoculars). By setting this scene properly, the other scenes can build properly. In the above example, the object seen could go from a bird to a flock of birds, to a flock of pterodactyls, to a portal to another dimension leading to the "Old Ones." The action could go from using binoculars, to huge telephoto lenses, to an observatory, to someone being omnipotent.

Pay attention to what is being built up so you can make use of the same objects, actions, and characters and build on them in your scene. Also keep in mind the things that are being heightened and make sure it's affecting your scene properly.

Variations

- You can include more than two teams in this game as they all get the same number of turns.
- Conversely, you can do this scene with a single team of actors who simply build upon their own scene.

39 Double Feature

For the emcee/teacher: Divide the group into two teams. Give each team a movie to reenact—completely—in 60 seconds. Both teams act out their "movie in a minute," and the audience chooses the winning movie. Choose movies that everyone knows well and have key scenes that are easy to recreate. *Titanic* is a good example: You have several scenes that can play out well, with the boat sinking being iconic.

You should also be in charge of the time. I find that it's best to call out "30 seconds," "15 seconds," and then give a 5-second countdown. It doesn't mess up the scene and will help the characters know when they need to wrap things up. It might sound like a cop-out, but ending the movie right when time is called will get a big pop from the crowd, and that's better than looking like you're making it easy on the actors. The opposite is that the actors have no idea they're out of time until the game is called and they find themselves nowhere near the end.

For the players: Go for big moments in the scene. In the *Titanic* example, hitting the iceberg at 30 seconds would be a good idea. That gives you time to work out the love story and still have the second half for the sinking.

Don't get caught up in long dialogue scenes. Often a few words will be enough. Sticking with the *Titanic* example, Jack and Rose can say "Hi" to each other and then go into the "King of the World" pose. That will be enough to communicate that they're together and still present another key movie scene.

40 Flashback

For the emcee/teacher: Divide the group into two teams. In this game, the first team on stage begins a basic scene. But soon into the scene, they will set up another one. This is done by saying things like, "This reminds me of the time…" or "Ever wonder about what happens when…?" or any other similar expression to segue from one scene to another. When they have set up the next scene, they will make the "flashback signal" (we use the old *Wayne's World* sign with the odd noise and hand movements). Once they do, the other team will come on stage and perform until they set up the next scene. This goes back and forth until the game is called.

For the players: While waiting to come on stage, pay attention to everything that is said. Once on stage, make sure you act on each point of the setup you've been given before setting up the scene you'll give the other team. Working on your scene is more important than working out what you'll give the other team to do.

And don't try to make the new setup too busy or too strange. Keep the scenes something that two or three actors can act out. And although bizarre is good, fun and simple work, too. I remember one scene in which an actor took a bite of a hot dog. "I wonder what it's like for that piece of hot dog right now," the other actor said. With that, the other team came on stage to act out hot dog going down the throat. Once in the stomach, it met other pieces of food and they talked while dissolving in stomach acid. Before the scene ended, the characters wondered how the human body was designed. This led to the other team acting like the R&D department of heaven, brainstorming the creation of humans. That led to an argument where they couldn't agree, and both man and woman were made.

Variation This game can work well as a fun long-form game.

41 Heckler Battle

Created in 1995, "Heckler Battle" was originally called "MST3K" after the TV show *Mystery Science Theater 3000*. In that game, one group of actors plays a scene completely serious, not going for laughs. The other actors watch the scene and make fun of it as if it were a bad movie. It's a game that I've now seen done all over the country.

Over the years, we realized that people like being the "Hecklers" in the scene, so we came up with a way for everyone to get that chance. "Heckler Battle" was born. In this game, the group is divided in two. One team begins their "serious" scene; and the other team sets out to heckle them. If the Hecklers can break the performing actors, making them laugh, they take the first team's place on stage, picking up the scene where it left off. The new group of Hecklers will then try to break the new actors. This continues until you call the scene.

The emcee will need to get a situation suggestion for this scene from the audience. It helps to ask for a serious situation, but I've found it even better to just get "one word of inspiration" for the scene and let the actors figure out their scene.

For the emcee/teacher: Divide the group into two teams.

For the players: Keep in mind that you need to move your scene along as much as you can. But as you do, you are also working out ways that the other actors can heckle you. This is the basic secret to the game. Giving a pause or making an action can be perfect for the other actors to heckle. Seasoned actors will find the right triggers to help their team and should try to set them into the scene.

Also, this game is not about "not breaking." You don't earn points by not laughing while on stage. Worse yet, the scene will get boring quickly. So if something strikes you as funny, go ahead and laugh. I love when the game has several swaps; that means it had a lot of laughs.

Quick Wits, as I mentioned, is a little more liberal about making fun of each other than some troupes. This game is the pinnacle of that. Although this works for us, be careful about doing it in your troupe unless every member is comfortable with it.

I performed this game with ComedySportz once and made this mistake. As one actor was looking for a basketball, another actor came onstage. This second actor was a large man, and I said, "I think I know what happened to the basketball." The audience laughed, but the actor was angry with me for the rest of the show, and it was obvious. After the show I was told, "We don't do that to each other in this troupe." I apologized and learned a big lesson.

42 Jip-Parody

For the emcee/teacher: This game is a variation of the game show *Jeopardy*. A quick Internet search will give you the background and style of the show. In our version, some actors will act as contestants while the remainder will serve as the category board. Give each member of the latter group a category for which they must give answers. The categories should be simple themes such as "things that start with the letter *s*," "ice cream flavors," "car parts," etc. You don't want categories that require long answers.

The contestants will then buzz in to give the question that goes with the answer. For the "buzzing in," just have the actors mime pushing a buzzer and making whatever noise they'd like. Each "answer" can have several "questions," and the contestants can buzz in until the emcee decides on a correct response.

The winner then picks a new category, and the game continues until the emcee calls the game. This can be done by either just calling for an end (usually on a particularly funny response) or by announcing that this is the final round, or "Final Jip-Parody."

Actors can all have a shot at it, or even give multiple answers until one is chosen as the correct answer. The game continues until the emcee decides it's gone long enough and calls a question as the "final category."

For the players: If you're part of the category board, you need to come up with answers that can be taken in different directions. This is why I like words with more than one syllable; they allow actors to break them up. The same can be said about answers with more than one word. Under "America" you could say, "bald eagle," and the correct question for that answer could be something like, "What is the most insecure member of the eagle family," or, "What do you get when you roll up an eagle?" See how the word *bald* was used differently? When I'm in charge of choosing the categories, I always make sure that I could give two answers to whatever I'm going to give the contestants.

As a contestant you need to break down that answer and find a way to make it work. One of my favorite answers was to "Napoleon." A contestant buzzed in and said, "What is the most comfortable type of linoleum." Now "Napoleon" and "Linoleum" don't end the same, but the sounds were close enough that it made sense that Napoleon was linoleum you could sleep on.

Take a moment to think about your answers, but it helps if someone is ready with a quick answer to buy some time. One of our actors, Joel Hilton, can somehow come up with an answer for anything instantly, and usually they're hilarious. But the key is that he'll buzz in quick to answer and that buys everyone else time to work out an answer.

Variations

- For teams with just a few actors on a given night, you can play this where everyone is a contestant and the whole audience is the category board. The actors will call out a category and let the crowd yell out their responses. The emcee will take the one that he thinks will work the best and give that to the contestants. Whichever actor wins that round will choose the next category.

- Another variation we use gives an actual "Final Jeopardy" ending. A new category is given by the emcee, who will also give the answer to it. The contestants will act as if they're writing down their answers, and the emcee will call "time." Then the emcee will go down the row asking what they wagered and what their answer is. It can be fun, but it's also hard for the last person in line. They have likely heard all the big answers given before it gets to them, so they'd better be ready with a few different answers.

43 Kangaroo Court

For the emcee/teacher: Divide the group into two teams. One team presents a scene, and the other team can lodge an "objection" about something that was said. As the emcee, you rule on it. If the objection is "sustained," the objecting team comes onstage and continues the scene in accordance to their objection. If it's "overruled," explain why the objection was overruled and have the scene continue as is.

For the players: Let the opening scene play a little bit so that it can establish the basic foundation. Pay attention to everything and be ready to object but be careful not to make this a game where you're objecting every three seconds. That quickly gets annoying.

Everything is open to objection: the actors on stage make a statement that isn't accurate, they stumble in their lines, someone walks through a piece of imagined scenery, etc.

Variation This game can be played by a small troupe. One person speaks on a subject, and the other actors can object to her presentation. If the emcee sustains the objection, the objecting actor takes over the lecture.

44 One-Word Debate

For the emcee/teacher: Divide the group into two teams. These two teams of actors will debate a topic, with a twist. Each member of a team will stand side by side and add only one word to the growing sentence. Once the end of the line is reached, the sentence can continue with the first actor. By adding one word at a time, the team has to find a way to complete the thought/argument. Team members can stop the sentence at any point; sometimes one word (like "No") is all you need.

As the emcee, you name a topic to start the debate. You might want to assign one team as in favor of the topic and the other against it. Start the debate by letting each side give an opening statement and then going back and forth from there. Ask specific questions of a side to make it seem more like a moderated debate.

For the players: This is one of the most basic improv games out there. All you have to do is listen to the others and keep things going. Don't try to lead too much; just get into the flow. Stay focused on the topic and your team's stance so that your scene will make sense.

Variation This game also works as a "Speak as One" scene. In this version, all of the actors on a team must speak at the same time, trying to get into a single mind-set and say the same thing. A key here is to start words slowly at first. Now make two teams and have them debate.

45 When Musicals Collide

For the emcee/teacher: Divide the group into two teams. Starting with a basic theme, each team creates a musical based on it. But it gets a little strange at the end.

The first team performs their musical's opening scene, usually including only one song. The second team follows with its opening scene. Each team then presents a second scene. Together, the teams now have four scenes done; it's time to "collide." The fifth scene must include both teams and both takes on the musical theme. This is where the musicals "collide."

The Fiddler from Oz

This last scene needs to wrap up both musicals and combine them in a logical fashion.

For the players: Your first scenes should be setups. If part of the first team, you can choose to do whatever you want within the theme. Those who are part of the second team have to do something different. In the second scenes, actors need to find common ground so that the musicals can combine in the fifth scene.

End the final scene with a big number that brings both musicals into play. This game can be the starting point for a fully improvised play.

46 Singles Bar

For the emcee/teacher: Divide the group into two teams. For this game we often bring up a woman from the audience to play the "target" for each team to pick up. Send one member from each team out. Then, with the audience, determine the type of man the woman is seeking: nationality, occupation, and physical feature. The challenge for the actors offstage is to be the first to come up with the correct combination.

Back on stage, the two "suitors" get help from the people at the bar (the other actors). Their conversations will provide clues, but teams can give clues only when the other team's person is on stage talking with the woman. This means that actors are trying to give clues to their player, hoping that the other team won't catch on to them. This game requires knowing one's teammates well.

The game ends when an actor correctly names all three details. You can award the game to the person who names all three parts or award points for each segment guessed correctly.

For the players: As an example, say that the woman is looking for a Norwegian accountant with big eyes. She (the audience volunteer) sits center stage with one of the actors trying to pick her up (we usually toss in bad pickup lines for fun). Players from the other team give clues to the woman's "ideal man" as they stand at the bar conversing. As a clue giver, remember that the clue is directed to your player and not the one on stage. You might say something like, "Did you hear that they're having problems in Europe?" Your companion responds, "No way!" trying to make "no way" sound like "Norway" but hoping that the other team's actor doesn't catch it.

A "suitor" might then announce that he's foreign and name a country. If he's right, the woman will react positively, and then he can try for the next detail. If he is wrong, she will turn her back to him, and he'll go away, opening the door for an actor from your team.

Always remember that it's a scene. Make the bar scene come alive, seeming like a real "meat market." When, as a suitor, you guess wrong, you should make mention of the incorrect first attempt when you come back next time. Work it like you might in real life.

47 Top That!

For the emcee/teacher: This game is all about physical movement and being aware of how movements look. Divide the group into two teams. Bring one actor from each team to the front and give one a simple action to perform. That actor will then perform the action—a golf swing for example—and keep repeating it. The other actor matches the action exactly. While they are doing the movement, the first actor says, "I'm hitting a golf ball; top that." The second actor must then come up with a different reason for the action. She might say something like, "Oh yeah? I'm doing the lamest dance move. Top that."

Play continues until one actor can't come up with something to say. Then a new actor replaces the losing actor, and you name a new activity. The new one should be very different from the first.

For the players: Think about what the action you're performing feels like, and what it looks like to others. Anything can work in this game, so don't be afraid to say something zany.

48 Five Seconds or Die!

For the emcee/teacher: Divide the group into two teams. One team chooses a member from the other team to do an impersonation of a famous person with a strange occupation. The impersonator will have five seconds to do the impersonation or "die." Once the actor has performed the impersonation, his team can challenge a member of the other team. Play goes back and forth until everyone has done an impersonation.

For the players: You don't have to be good at impersonations for this game; you just have to come up with something quickly. So don't sweat it; just act.

The comedy of this game comes from the challenges given and the attempts to perform them, so come up with some strange impersonation suggestions. Just don't give someone a person she wouldn't know to impersonate.

49 Hitchhiker

For the emcee/teacher: This is one of the first games I teach actors to help them work on character. For some reason it remains an audience favorite.

Divide the group into two teams. Arrange four chairs in two rows of two, creating a "car with seats for four." There should be two members of each team in the car, and they should not be next to each other. To ensure this order, think of the seating as a circle; keep everyone separated by a member of the opposite team.

Give the four actors a character type to act out as they "ride" in the car. Play goes on this way until another actor steps up as the "hitchhiker." The hitchhiker should be from the opposite team of the person in the front passenger seat. The actors in the car call out, "Hitchhiker!" The driver stops the car and gets out, and the remaining three actors rotate clockwise, leaving the front passenger seat open. The new actor takes that seat and starts up a new character, which the other three immediately adopt.

This continues until you feel they've had enough changes and hit a good high point. The game is good for practice at creating instant character types.

For the players: Go big on the characters; you're only going to do each of them for a short time. Interact with the others in the car, creating a mini-scene.

If you play the hitchhiker, make sure that you come in strong with your character. The others in the car will want to jump into whatever you're giving them, so make sure that it's obvious right up front. As an example, one night an actor came into the scene very quietly. Everyone thought he was a mime and started doing "mime" things. The actor stopped the scene, saying that he was acting out a "shy" person. Now the scene was ruined; we had nowhere to go. It's a good example of the importance of coming in with a big character, and an even better example of why not to pull back the curtain and tell the audience what you were "trying to do." If they can't figure out what you are—you've only got yourself to blame.

Variation This game doesn't have to be a competition. Let the whole group play, with all actors lining up to play hitchhikers.

50 Town Hall

For the emcee/teacher: Divide the group into two teams. For this game, the actors find seats in the audience. Acting as town mayor, you bring a problem before this town hall meeting, opening it for discussion. The actors, playing concerned citizens, pop up as a little debate begins.

Have one team represent one side of the issue and another team take the opposite side. Often this isn't decided up front; it just comes down to whoever speaks first and the side she takes. The rest of her team will then fall into place.

As the scene continues, give the floor to the actors as they ask for it and try to moderate the meeting as best you can. The audience can decide the winner.

For the players: You can do so much with this game. You can create such interesting characters, and playing the scene from the audience gives it an extra dimension, especially when you use audience members as part of your character's story. I have played a scout leader who has brought his troupe with him, and I introduce them. Now they are "with me," and I can do little things with that. I've also been a polygamist leader with his wives (one of them was an obvious male), I've been a coach with his team, and I've been a stay-at-home father with his kids. But even the single characters are fun.

The point is, many characters will work in this setting. No matter how crazy you make them, they just have to fit somewhere into the city.

Pay close attention to what the actors at the meeting are saying; bring up a counterpoint or information to help prove your point.

51 Rap Battle

Music Preferably a repetitive hip-hop beat without words

For the emcee/teacher: Divide the group into two teams. This game is a rhyming battle between the two teams. Begin by picking a word that the actors have to rhyme and give them a musical beat to go behind their rap. The teams will then pick a "front person," with the others acting as back-up singers.

The first front person begins a rap. Her lines end in words that rhyme with the assigned word but do not use it. The back-up singers fill in the blanks, saying the word in unison or losing a point. For example, let's say that "shoe" was the chosen word. The team's lead might say something like, "I've got a cow, and he says, ___." The back-up rappers yell, "Moo!" Now the other team has to respond, "I've gotta favorite color, and it is ___." "Blue!"

A team failing to complete the rhyme loses the round and has to rotate to a different front person. The game is over after all of the front people on one team have lost.

For the players: Practice the rap. Get the rhythm down and remember that you need only a few words. Also don't try to be too clever; that usually trips up a team. The idea is to try to have a long battle, not just the coolest rhymes.

Line-Up Games

These games are a closer cousin to stand-up than true improv comedy. The player's job is to come up with a joke quickly and step up to deliver it.

Tell your group that, for these games, their time on stage is going to be short. Remind them to bring a strong presentation, believe that they're delivering "gold," and present it as such. I've seen players step up timidly, give their line half-heartedly, and then slink away. Then they wonder why they don't get laughs.

On the other side, I've seen actors step up, deliver a line as if it was Comedy Hall of Fame material, and then stand there daring the audience not to laugh. Whether it was a great line or not, they usually get something in return. And when they don't get laughs, they toss it off and get back in line with the same confidence.

Caution actors against trying to explain their jokes on the assumption that the audience didn't get it. Most likely, the audience did get it; they just didn't want it. Also, coach them not to spend too much time trying to make a joke work. If it doesn't come quickly, it's time to move on to something else.

Some of this section's other games involve putting players in a line not to deliver a joke but to continue a story or create a short scene. Encourage players to go full out for those few seconds, get ready for the next opportunity, and keep their eyes and ears open at all times.

52 Scenes from a Hat

Props A box or hat containing several scene ideas written on slips of paper

For the emcee/teacher: This game can be played a few different ways, but this is the "Freeze Tag" version. Start with two actors on stage. Give them a starting scene and let them act it out for a short time before calling "Freeze." The two actors freeze in position, and then two other actors tag them and take their positions, remaining frozen. Create a new scene for the actors, who must justify the strange frozen positions from which they start the scene. You can play this as a group game with actors just jumping in or as a team vs. team game in which each new scene is made up of members of the other team.

Make sure that you call for the freeze when it works best for the scene. Often this is when something physical is happening on stage. Watch closely so you can catch the right moment.

Have a wide scene selection from which to draw and keep them basic, often just a simple action like mowing the lawn. As you play this game, you'll get a feel for the types of suggestions that work, and you can create a "box" of ideas that fits your troupe.

For the players: To help the scene, make sure that you're physical in this one. This doesn't mean that you need to get into big hug or wrestling holds or jump on each other all the time. You can do big gestures with your arms, mime working with large objects, or act as if you're pulling or pushing something. Such movements can get overlooked in this game, but they are great for finding "Freeze" moments.

The other element of this game is the justification of the position you're in at the beginning of the scene. Take a moment before starting the scene to figure out the best way to continue. I find that it's best to do this while you're moving in to make the tag. And if one actor starts explaining the position from another rationale, go with it. It doesn't matter if you had a better idea; their reality has already been built.

Variation This game can be played very well in teams. The teams alternate coming on stage and setting up bizarre freeze positions for the other team to deal with in their scene.

53 Catchphrase

For the emcee/teacher: Have the players line up on the stage. Give them a made-up superhero name (either from audience suggestions or your own list). The actors then step forward one at a time and give you that hero's catchphrase. Keep an eye on the actors, and you'll know when they are done with a hero name. You should call out another made-up superhero then.

For the players: In games like this, puns are your friend. This game provides a good opportunity to practice wordplay. And make sure to sell your phrase like it's coming from a superhero. Strike poses and use other means to help you.

Variation This game can be played competitively, with the audience deciding which team has the best phrases. Or change it up slightly by asking for super villain catchphrases.

54 Caruso

Prop A pair of sunglasses

For the emcee/teacher: We created this game during the first season of *CSI: Miami* because we loved the way David Caruso made little puns about death in the opening of the show. The TV show's writers abandoned that when everyone caught on to the joke, but we've built that into this game, which remains popular.

Give the actors a public location for a murder scene. The actors then come up with David Caruso–type lines to open the episode. Using our sound improviser, we play the familiar scream from the opening music (The Who's "Won't

Get Fooled Again") after each delivery. It adds to the game. If you don't have that piece ready, you can have all the other actors make the "Yeeeeaaaaah!" scream; you'll probably get some of the audience to join you.

For the players: Watch *CSI: Miami* episodes online to get an idea of Caruso's delivery. Mimic how he places his hands on his hips or how he puts on his sunglasses. Capture his pauses just right. He'll usually do one of these before the pun.

For example, let's use the suggested location of an "art gallery." An actor comes up to the front, looks at the body on the floor with his hands on his hips and says, "Well, it looks like this killer might have been *framed*." The actor then puts on sunglasses just as he finishes the line, and the scream comes in. Other lines might have been: "Okay, boys, time to *canvas* the scene," or, "Looks like a robbery gone bad. Somebody stole all his *Monet*," or…okay, I could do this all day.

Variation This can be played as a team game.

55 Dance Craze

Music Dance music

For the emcee/teacher: Backed by fun dance music playing, the actors will perform dances inspired by various occupations or objects.

As with most games, make sure your watch the players to know when to change the subject. They won't like it if you stay on a subject they feel they've exhausted.

For the players: Think about the movements that someone doing a certain job would make every day. Now put that action to a musical beat and turn it into a dance. It helps to repeat some actions over and over to make it seem more like a dance.

Bring in other actors to help create the dance. If the suggestion was "dentist" you might bring out another actor as your "patient" and mime pulling her teeth. When set to music, the tug of war between you could look like a dance.

56 Screen Test

For the emcee/teacher: Given a well-known movie, actors present a failed audition for a role in it. This often includes the impersonation of a famous actor who really wouldn't have auditioned. This game calls for big movies with iconic characters, such as *Star Wars*. Imagine all the different actors who might have auditioned for Darth Vader!

For the players: This game is good for troupes of actors who can do impersonations, but don't despair if you can't do voices well. You can still play. Sometimes you can get by with a weak voice just by announcing the name of the person. You might say, "I'm Pee-wee Herman, and I'll be auditioning for the role of Darth Vader." You're likely to get a decent laugh.

But since we're talking about impersonations, let's talk about how to come up with them. Doing an impersonation is not much different from doing an accent. You will come to them more quickly if you stick with the stereotypes first and expand from there. William Shatner is a perfect example. People don't do Shatner impressions anymore; they do impressions of Shatner impressions. His halts were never as dramatic as they seem in countless impressions. But by doing just a few of them and saying that you're Shatner, you've got an impression.

Work on a few that you can do and be ready to bring them out in this game. The best part is you only need to say a few words and it's over. Just make the most of those few words.

57　Taglines

For the emcee/teacher: This game is based on an impression of Arnold Schwarzenegger and his "unique" acting style. Moreover, it's based on his old movies in which he'd kill a bad guy and then immediately make a pun.

Give the actors an object that you wouldn't normally think of as a weapon. They must use it "Arnold" style, giving the death pun at the end.

For the players: Arnold is almost like Shatner; it's an impression that most people can do. Just stick to the stereotypes of the impression, and you'll do fine. Remember: you're actually doing an impression of the impression.

When you perform, I find that it's better to make a motion as if you've just used the "weapon" before making the pun. Then just deliver your line. If "banana" was the object, you might say, "Now you can split," "Your death will have a peel," "Ooh, it looks like you bruise easily," or even, "Orange you glad I used a banana?"

Variation　You can also use occupations with this game. You might try mixing objects and occupations.

58　Back in My Day

For the emcee/teacher: Actors comment on a particular modern convenience, acting as if they are old. They might say, "Back in my day, we didn't have [blank]," and then explain what they did instead. Each actor will have a chance to give his line.

Get modern items for actors to use, but you can play the game with less modern things as well. It makes the actor sound really old if they say, "Back in my day, we didn't have shoes. We tied cats to the bottoms of our feet, and we were grateful."

For the players: It's good to sell the fact that you're old. A little shakiness in your voice or your walk will help. Making an effort will go a long way to making the game successful.

It's okay to come up with strange things that the older generation "used to do" (like the cat example above). Most young people think that older people exaggerate how it was in the old days anyway, so go with it. You also can go with angry type answers such as, "Back in my day, we didn't have Facebook. If you wanted to know how someone was, you ASKED them!" Think about what you might do if you didn't have the given item and then push your thinking.

59 Connect the Dots

For the emcee/teacher: This is a strange little scene-building game that actually doesn't build a scene. Instead it builds the tableau of the scene.

Name an inanimate object and have one of the actors strike the pose of the object, proclaiming that she is that item. The other actors will build onto this, one at a time, until everyone is in the scene.

Once this is done, select (or have the audience select) one player from the scene. That actor repeats his pose and, again, the other actors will add to it, creating something very different from the previous scene.

For the players: Get creative with "what works" with a given object. If the first person is a lamp, you could be the bulb, the power cord, the lampshade, the person reading next to the lamp, the man stealing the lamp, the lightning bolt that will cause a power surge and blow up the lamp, or whatever you'd like.

You can create fun scenes off of this. If you went with the lightning bolt, the next actor could be Zeus tossing the bolt at an annoying fly. Then someone could be that fly. The "dots" don't have to make immediate sense; it's as they get connected that things work out.

Variation This game can be used as the start to a long-form. The items connecting the dots can help establish the themes that the long-form can explore.

60 Talk Talk

For the emcee/teacher: Have a small group of actors line up in front of you. As you point at one of them, she will talk about a subject that either you or the audience has supplied. The actor will continue to talk until you point to another actor who will pick up the story exactly where the first one left off. This will continue until the scene ends.

You can change up the scene as much as you want simply by moving to different actors. After a bit of practice, you will realize that you can actually control the scene because you'll know in what direction particular actors might take a scene.

This game teaches the actors to watch and listen. They will stay focused on you to see when it might be their turn to talk. They will also listen to the actors around them so that they'll be able to keep a story going instantly when it comes to them. Use this game in rehearsals and warm-ups to get the mind flowing.

For the players: You have to be engaged in this game the entire time. Keep an eye on the emcee. Often he will give little clues that he's about to turn to you. Also, listen closely to the story and be thinking about it, so that you stay up to speed with the flow. Be ready to continue the plot but don't pre-think where you're going to take it when it comes to you. If you're busy thinking about what you're going to do, you can't be listening to what is happening right now.

Variation "Talk or Die" is played just like the game above, except if a player doesn't come in immediately, repeats the previous word ("He went to the"—"the store"), or says something unrelated to what was just said, he is out. The audience yells, "Die!" to let the actor know that he is out. For more fun, have the "dead" player act out his death for the audience.

61 Ranting Hot Spot

For the emcee/teacher: Give one actor a subject that would be hard to "rant" about, such as kittens. The actor will immediately talk about why she doesn't like the subject. The other actors will be behind this actor; one of them will tap the first "ranter" out, take her place, and begin a rant based on something he heard the first actor say.

This continues, with each actor tagging out the actor before him and then giving his rant, until the game is called. The hidden skill that this game teaches is how to heighten a scene. Each new rant usually brings new energy and emotion to the stage. Actors can use that same skill to give more excitement to a scene.

For the players: Be listening for key words in other actors' rants that can trigger you. Remember: you're not going to rant about the same thing that the previous actor did; you're gong to rant about something that that person *said*. This is important to this game because you want to see where it all leads to when it's done. You might start with kittens, but it's unlikely that you'll end up anywhere close.

Variation This game can be played musically in a variation we call "Musical Hot Spot": One actor starts singing a song and then one of the other players can tap that actor out and sing the song that comes to their mind. This continues around and around. One way to end the game is to have the actor who sang the first song come back up again with that same song. Alternatively, you can end on a song that brings in all the actors to sing together.

62 Oscar Scene

Props Two containers, one filled with fake movie titles and one with different roles/occupations

For the emcee/teacher: In this game, call each actor to the front one at a time and give her one role/occupation and one fake movie title. The actor must immediately do her "Oscar Scene" based on that information. Play until each actor has had a turn.

Have a good mix of movie titles and roles, and you'll be amazed at the great combinations that will come from this. We've had some truly great monologues come from playing this game. Although most are done for fun, many of the actors take this game to heart and try to do the best they can, even with a combination like "the steel worker" in "Hey, Don't Tickle Me."

For the players: Remember that these scenes are typical of those shown at the Oscars to introduce a nominee. Act it out with everything you've got. Cry, yell, throw your body around, whatever it takes to have your "Oscar Moment."

Variation We let the audience decide who gets the Oscar after all the actors have done their scene. Then we make that actor give an acceptance speech (which we usually cut short).

Musical Games

I've already spoken at length about musical games so all I really want to do is remind you that shorter is better. Keep your lyrics light, and you'll have less chance of messing up the rhythm. Keep your choruses short and use just a few words; other actors will be able to join in, and you won't have to struggle to keep it going.

Note All of these games require some sort of musical accompaniment. Ideally you should have someone who can perform the music live—pianos or guitars work best. There is no need to have a full band, but if you have one, go for it. If you can't provide live accompaniment, you can try instrumental tracks, but doing so forces the actor to sing whatever is given to them, rather than giving them the flexibility that comes from working with live musicians.

63 Broadway Musical Writers

Music Live accompaniment, if possible (see the Note just above)

For the emcee/teacher: Two actors portray writers of a new Broadway musical. Give them a topic for the musical and let them go to work. As they talk about the show they want to write, they'll discuss certain scenes and songs. As they set them up, the scenes/songs are then performed by the other actors on the stage.

The "writers" should lay out the story so that it flows like an actual show (beginning to end). Start with the opening number and work your way to the big ending song. I would suggest only three to four scenes/songs for this game.

For the players: As one of the writers for this game, you must come up with a plot structure for the musical and convey it as though brainstorming. Give the other actors good material to perform. If you give them stuff that is too hard, you will hurt the scene.

If you're one of the performers, you should know that you're not doing a full scene, just a part of one. That being said, you can pick up the scene right before the song is going to begin. A few lines leading up to the song will be good enough to get things across. Pay close attention to what the writers are saying so that you can make the scene look like what they imagined.

Both writers and performers need to make sure that the ending wraps up everything nicely. Give the song a big ending with all the performers singing.

Variation This game can be played without the music; then the writers can be putting a movie together. Or they can be movie reviewers and set up scenes from the movie they are reviewing.

64 Greatest Hits

Music Live accompaniment, if possible (see the Note on page 86)

For the emcee/teacher: This game is a knockoff of television commercials for compilation CDs. One to three actors portray the actors talking about the album, while another small group (or solo performer) sings the featured songs.

Name a theme for the compilation. This can be anything, such as an occupation, that you normally wouldn't associate with music. The commercial starts with the actors talking about the offer. They then set up each song, saying something like, "And it includes my all-time favorite hit, [song title]." At this point, the song is sung.

The game usually includes three songs. We try to end the game on a big song. You can have it end by going back to the actors with an "Act now" type of message/ending, but you'll probably find the crowd will be applauding the singing, so that can be the ending.

For the players: As with most games, if you're setting up others to sing, don't go for the joke. You'll mess them up. Singing is hard enough without having to make a song out of your joke. Also, don't

put too much into your description of the song or the song title. Give the singers some wiggle room, or they will be limited in what they can do. Lastly, don't use the best joke in your song title. It may hamper the singers.

As the singer, work using the "List Method." As soon as you hear the topic, start thinking of everything you might connect with it and begin compiling your list of rhymes. You'll have a little time while the actors set up the commercial premise; use it.

Variation This game can be played with all the actors on stage together, like a band doing their own commercial. Have the crowd name both the band and the theme of their new album. Then the actors will set up their own songs. This is sort of like a press conference with the audience as the "press." We've had the band ask them for some of their favorite songs they'd like to hear, or even just a question about their upcoming tour.

65 Lounge Singer

Music Live accompaniment, if possible (see the Note on page 86)

For the emcee/teacher: Give a small group of actors (we usually have one or two singers) a location where they've been hired to entertain as "lounge singers." The location is usually a place where you would least expect to see this type of entertainment.

The actors then banter before going into their songs. As they do the setup, they give it a little backstory and the title. Again, this is hokey Vegas we're talking about here.

For the players: I like to have two actors play the entertainers because it allows them to play off each other. They can also set each other up for the songs. We also like to make our keyboard player a part of the act and talk to him from time to time. It adds to the "show" that you're putting on.

Make yourselves seem as if you're "big time." Don't act as if this gig is beneath you, but rather put on an air that everyone knows you and is excited to have you here. Feel free to talk to the crowd a little bit as if they are all workers (or whatever) at the location. Having fun within the location will really sell the game.

66 Sounds Like a Song Title

Music Live accompaniment, if possible (see the Note on page 86)

For the emcee/teacher: This game plays out like a musical. Listen to the scene, and when you hear something said that sounds good, announce, "That sounds like a song title." The song immediately begins, and the last thing said becomes the song title or theme.

Find the right moments to jump in. Do it quickly because the actors might be wrapped up in their scene and already be continuing. I find that it helps to announce the line again so that everyone is clear as to the song title.

Don't try to ram songs too close together. Let the scene develop a little so you can see where the actors are going, or even what new characters might come in. The scene will usually have about three songs; hopefully you'll get a good one from the group and can end on a high note.

For the players: You can do a little cheating here. Knowing that the emcee is going to call a song on good lines, you can lead her to call what you'd like. You also can lead the scene into themes that are easy for you to sing about. But the best advice is simply to be ready—your emcee could call out anything for this game.

Variation This game can be done as a competition between two actors. One actor says a line that "sounds like a song title," and the other actor that has to sing it.

Improv Magic Moment: The Singing Battle

I was in the finals of a statewide Improv Survivor with Shawn Zumbrunnen (who has beaten me twice!), and the final game was the game variation I just spoke of above. I was a little bummed; Shawn is easily the best musical improviser I've worked with. We're good friends, but he knew he had me. I could see it in his eyes as well. But then the variation was mentioned: I would be setting up the song title for Shawn to sing. I had a plan.

The scene played like a normal scene until I unleashed my attack. I said something to the effect of, "It's like you always say...everything looks better purple and orange." Shawn instantly knew what I had done, and he glanced at the emcee. Unfortunately the host didn't call the obvious setup. Shawn gave me a little smile knowing that he'd dodged a bullet, but it didn't end there. What followed was the two of us battling back and forth trying to give the other a song title with a ridiculous word to rhyme.

The audience caught on and was laughing at the duel, but, oddly enough, the emcee never realized what was happening. Eventually he called out for a title of a very easy setup, and we went back to singing. But that little battle will always be one of my favorite moments. And, yes, Shawn won.

67 Bad Beatnik Poetry

Music Live accompaniment, if possible (see the Note on page 86)

For the emcee/teacher: For this game, give the actors a theme. Have them create a poem and sing it beatnik style. The style is hard to describe in a book, but you can find examples online or just create your own. The rhyming scheme is AABB, but the first line starts with one word being repeated. Here's an example of the flow:

> Bob, Bob
> Writing a book.
> Hoping you will stop and take a look.
> Inside he knows you're sure to find,
> Something that will just blow your mind.

The next person's section must start with the word *mind*, but it can go anywhere.

> Mind, mind
> I sure do not
> That's why I got in trouble a lot.
> My parents say I'll go to jail one day,
> But until then I'm going to play.

Play keeps going until everyone's had a chance or you feel that the game's gone on long enough. We often use this game for birthdays or occasions when we want to bring someone up on stage and make the song about him or her.

If you have a drummer in the group, he will add a lot by keeping the beat with brushes on a snare drum. We've also added a saxophone background for more production value.

For the players: This game can be fun to work in the most bizarre things. I wrote the example above to show you that one section doesn't have to follow the other in theme. You just have to use the last word from the previous actor as your starting word. Wait for that word and see what comes to mind. This is good practice for free-flowing rhyme.

But if you do this with someone you bring up on stage, I'd have the poetry focus on her. Gather a few details about her and work them into your beatnik poetry.

68   Musical Chairs

Props Chairs

Music Live accompaniment, if possible (see the Note on page 86)

For the emcee/teacher: Yes, this game actually has your actors playing the "Musical Chairs" kids' game, but it has a twist.

Get suggestions from the audience about songs they'd like to hear. Then set your actors in motion by playing music and having them walk around the chairs. (I'm assuming that you remember how to play the original "Musical Chairs.") When the music stops, the actor who doesn't get a seat has to sing a song based on one of the audience suggestions.

This continues until only one actor remains, and he wins. This is a fun way to get in some songs without having to rely on a scene setup. Also it's fun to see people play musical chairs in front of an audience.

For the players: This is a fun game; don't sweat the whole "chair" thing. Just be ready to sing.

69   Singing Psychiatrist

Music Live accompaniment (see the Note on page 86)

For the emcee/teacher: The setup for this game is that the singing psychiatrist makes his patients sing their problems to him, and he sings back the treatment. Often the two work into a duet by the end of the session. We usually have a couple of patients per game; when the first is done, the doctor may ask an assistant to bring in the next.

Start by getting audience suggestions for a few "problems" that the patients may have. These can be anything that a person might see a psychiatrist about, including all sorts of fears. The "patients," just off stage, have a little time to think through a song. They come on stage one at a time. The game ends when all patients have been treated.

For the players: As a patient, you have a little time to create your song. The first patient will have the least time, so your most experienced singer takes the lead spot. Sing about your problem and how it's hurting you; remember that you're talking to a doctor and needing help.

As the doctor, you'll have a little foreknowledge of the troubles coming your way but not exactly how they'll be presented. As the patient is singing, listen for words to jump out at you. If you need a little time before you sing, stall by talking to the patient when her song is done, maybe asking a few questions. Don't stall too long, however. Remember: You're the singing psychiatrist, not the talking one.

Variation Set the game in a bar and have a bartender asking customers about their troubles. This variation can be played much the same way as the original game, but customers sing their answers, and the bartender sings back to them.

70 Scene to Rap

Music Simple "hip hop" music with a strong beat and ideally no words (optional)

For the emcee/teacher: Get simple scene or location suggestions from the audience. Then have the actors perform the entire scene as if it were a rap.

Doing a "Scene to Rap" will scare a few actors, but have them try it a few times in rehearsal. They'll see that it can be a lot easier than they think. The idea is that you can basically do something that you'd find within the pages of Dr. Seuss, and if it's got a rap beat behind it, you can make it work.

The actors will still need to have characters and form a scene. A rap scene should lead pretty easily to a confrontation because the actors will use the rhymes in a "battle" style almost instinctively. Hopefully they bring it to a resolution, and you can end the scene.

For the players: Play with the genre. Some actors will do some beat box and others will do some "scratching" noises in their raps; the crowd will love that. Listen to some of the music and note patterns such as repeated words or hitting the key words extra hard.

Play to your strengths here. If you can do the rap style, go for it. If not, see what you can bring. Can you dance? Can you walk with rapper attitude? Anything you can bring to the table can be used here. Even if you're just the guy in the background who keeps shouting, "What? What?" you can add to the scene.

On Your Toes

One of my favorite parts of doing an improv show is the constant change that can happen. Something about arriving at the theater and having no idea what you're going to do appeals to me.

The games in this section will test your mind and change things up throughout the performance. These games push you to focus on being in the moment. If you can make your way through these, you can do just about anything.

71 Scene in Reverse   · ·

For the emcee/teacher: Only a few actors will play this game with any confidence; I'm always grateful when I've got a few who will play it with me.

Start the scene from the end and work your way backward to the beginning. You don't have to speak backward; you just need to perform the lines and actions in the reverse order. This means actors must pay close attention to what was said before you. Many scenes get messed up by an actor coming on stage and saying "hi." That seems innocent, but it will cause the other actors to have to find a way to cover this and keep the scene moving. I've fixed the above example by saying, "I know you're about to leave, but first tell me if you think the price of gas is too high or too low." Not genius, but it worked.

For the players: It's best to start with a freeze that looks like something big has happened and then reveal how it happened. Many of our scenes start with someone lying on the ground, and we go from there.

Be on the lookout for lines that actors might say that are actually responses to lines that you've just said. This would be inaccurate, and you'll have to adjust to it.

Be careful. This game will stick with you; you'll be thinking about it during your next game.

72 Fortune Cookie

Props Fortune cookies

For the emcee/teacher: Give the actors a basic scene to perform. Then spread fortune cookies around the front of the stage or hand one to each actor. The actors begin the scene, as usual, but along the way, each of them must open at least one cookie and read the fortune out loud. When they do, they know what must happen during this scene.

It's best that the actors not open the cookies as the scene begins because the action can get chaotic. I let them build the scene a little and then reveal the fortunes one at a time. The scene ends when all the fortunes have been worked out.

For the players: Just because you've read your fortune doesn't mean that you're going to make it come true. You should take on an air of disbelief about the fortune you receive, seeming skeptical that it will come true. It's up to the other actors to devise a way to make the fortune work out. This adds another layer to the game.

Variation This game can be played by using horoscopes instead of fortune cookies.

73 The Gauntlet

For the emcee/teacher: This game is actually three games in one. Decide on three games that the actors will play and in what order they will be called. The actors receive their setup and begin a normal scene.

After everything is set in place with the scene, call out the first game. The actors then put the rules of that game into the scene. After that game has run its course, call the next one. The actors shift to that game's style, and the same thing will happen for the last game.

The order of the games should lead up to the hardest being performed last. This will get the actors and audience comfortable with what is happening before hitting them with the big one.

For the players: This game can be played up like it's really hard, but in truth, it's just a fun way to get in three games. Often the chosen games are the type that don't work well for more than a minute. Games such as "Questions" (speaking only in questions) or "Song Lyrics" (speaking only in song lyrics) are perfect for one of the sections.

Keep the scene going with whatever is thrown at you. It's fun to see how the different games can sway a scene. And be ready for a swap to come at any point in the game. Don't get too comfortable in a certain style.

Variation When a new game is announced, have the actors combine its rules with that of the previous game. When the third game is called, see if the troupe can deal with all three rules at once.

74 Film Noir

For the emcee/teacher: This game is based on old detective movies that sometimes used inner monologues to convey information. In this version, as the actors perform a scene, they can step forward (freezing the other actors) and share their thoughts. This often affects the scene and the actions of the other actors.

For the "detective" aspect of this game, we ask the audience for a movie title, prompting them with. "The Case of the Missing [blank]." One actor plays the detective; another is the person needing help (preferably a femme fatale). A third actor can be anything from an assistant to a criminal. Play continues until the situation is resolved or has deteriorated into craziness.

For the players: Play the scene like its genre. In the movies, the detective was ultra cool and tough. He spoke slowly and with purpose. The women were beautiful and almost purred when they talked. Find your groove in the scene and play it out fully.

This game lets you force your fellow players into strange predicaments. In an inner monologue, you might say, "She's beautiful, sure, but what really impressed me was when she broke into that crazy Michael Jackson impersonation," or "He doesn't know it yet, but I've filled his pants with itching powder. It should take effect any moment." These are fun to do, but be aware that the other players can do the same to you.

Variation The game works even better if you can supply a little background music to fit the mood. Some slow saxophone or jazz music hits the spot.

75 Hidden Agenda

For the emcee/teacher: This game is similar to "Film Noir" (Game #74), but it can be played in any genre or period. Another difference is that the actors don't give their own inner thoughts—you, as the emcee, give them.

Make a trigger signal or ask your sound improviser to play something to alert actors to the coming inner monologue. When this is heard, an actor steps forward to find out what his or her character is thinking. Although it's an inner monologue, the other actors of course hear it. They can work with the knowledge; their challenge is to do it in a naïve way. The actors should take turns stepping out so that they never go twice in a row.

You can also use this device to let the characters leak little secrets about themselves. Having an actor step up to reveal "I have a crush on Dora the Explorer," or "I shouldn't have eaten that extra burrito" can lead to strange twists as well. As emcee, you want to pay close attention to the scene to either complicate it or find ways to put the characters in conflict with each other.

For the players: As stated, your challenge is to work with your hidden agenda—even though everyone knows about it. You also need to find ways to mess up your scene partner's plans in a way that feels like you don't know about the plans. If through a "hidden agenda" you heard that someone is planning to rob you of your watch, you might suddenly lock your watch in a safe. You can work to thwart other characters, but you have to do that without any sort of thought that someone wants to take the watch. That's what makes this game so twisted.

76 Accents

For the emcee/teacher: This game is a fairly common game in troupes. The actors start a normal scene but, as it continues, you call out various accents for them to use, changing the scene as the accent might dictate.

It's a simple premise, but your actors go through many different accents until the scene is done, and that is tough. I like to start the game with more simple accents (which accents that includes depends on which your actors are good at performing). This allows the actors to get comfortable and build the scene. And as you call, make sure that the accent you call is different from the previous one, from Scottish to French for example. But don't go British to Australian. England and Australia don't have the same accents, but they might be close enough that the actors will have a hard time. It's easier for the actors if the switch is extreme.

For the players: The key to any accent is finding a word or phrase that helps you sink into that voice. Usually, that's a stereotype such as "Crikey" for Australian, "Nein!" for German, or "Sacre bleu!" for French. Make that the first thought that comes to mind before you speak.

Keep the scene moving along through the accent change but don't be afraid to let the accent shift the flow a little. I've seen very hectic scenes put on the brakes when "Jamaican" was called. It's the attitude associated with the accent that can often change the pace and, with it, the scene. Just keep the basics in place and let it flow.

Variation In the variation called "Emotions," players constantly change emotions instead of accents. This game is easier than "Accents" for young players, because everyone can get a handle on emotions. Encourage the actors to imagine what in the situation might make them feel the called-for emotion and then keep the scene going. Make sure they know to go BIG on the emotions.

You can also play this game with "Film and Theater Styles," "Occupations," "Magazines," etc. The quick change of this style is great for many things. See what works for you.

77 Time Machine

For the emcee/teacher: As actors perform their scene, you, as emcee, call various time shifts. The actors will instantly jump to that point in the scene. These can be jumps of a few seconds or minutes or jumps of years. Time can jump forward or back.

You drive the scene. If two actors are talking about doing something that might take some time, jump to the end of that time to see what happens. If they are talking about a fight, jump a few minutes ahead to see who wins. As you practice this game, you'll see the direct correlation between the changes in the time and the direction of the scene.

As a bonus, you can always call everything back to "present day." This is almost like a reset button, and you can use it to get a scene back on track.

For the players: You need to be ready to jump in at any time, but you also can help dictate where the scene goes by the things you say. Announce a time for something, and, more than likely, the emcee will jump to that time to see what you were thinking. As an example, if you say, "I remember when I met you three years ago" the emcee is likely to call "Three years ago" for the time shift and have you act that out. The more you play this game, the more you'll see that teamwork with the emcee has a great payoff.

78 Raise the Bar

For the emcee/teacher: The fun of this game comes from having the stakes raised again and again. Starting simply, the scene quickly changes when you give a signal (a buzzer, bell, anything), alerting the actors to "raise the bar."

As an example, say the scene has two actors digging a hole. When the signal is given, one actor yells, "We've struck oil!" The scene has a new element added to it, and the characters will have to deal with the oil. If the signal sounds again, the other actor might then say, "The oil is coming too fast," and then both begin flailing, as if swimming in oil.

This game will help train actors to make a scene more interesting—or to deal with it when thrown a big curve. This game can work for beginners, but you'll find that advanced players can really get creative with it.

For the players: If it's your turn to raise the bar, say the first thing that comes to mind. Really great things happen when you don't think too much and just go with the flow. But do make sure that everyone gets a chance to raise the bar. You don't want to hog the scene. And regardless of who initiates the change, everyone should react big to a new situation. Remember, this game is about raising the bar, so you need to play that up.

Re-Scene Games

This next list of games all have the simple theme of seeing a scene repeated (sometimes more than once) but with new twists added. Both actors and audience enjoy these games because they have a foundation to work from after the first presentation.

A strength of these games is that they allow the actors to re-examine what they did before. This might not be apparent to the audience right away because the actors do the scene differently each time, but the actors know and benefit from the opportunity.

You'll see that some of the games on the list ask for the re-scene to be done completely differently, while others will want the new scene to come as close to the original as the players can make it with the slight changes. Actors should keep up on what the scene is looking for and follow the setup of the game; the quick joke is not the challenge here.

79 Deaf Replay

This game requires 4 actors; 1 of whom can be an audience member.

For the emcee/teacher: In this game, two people do a scene while two others watch it but can't hear anything that is said. The second group of actors then tries to recreate the scene based only on what they think the actions were telling them about the scene. When doing this as a performance game, we generally bring someone up from the audience to be in the first scene.

Give the actors a basic scene, but pick one that will have a lot of action to it. If you bring up an audience member make sure that they know you want them to make grand gestures. The more that is done in the scene the better it will be for the second group to try and re-create it. The first scene should run only 60 to 90 seconds long. If it runs longer, it will be harder for the other actors to remember all the action. Remember to keep the second group of actors from hearing the scene. We go with the low budget way of sticking our fingers in our ears and wiggling them.

For the players: The first group should perform the scene they are given without making it obvious what it is through the actions. If your scene is a rodeo, you don't want to jump right into the cowboy stuff. A few other actions first may throw the second group off and allow them to create something new.

Also, find ways to go over the top. If you're going to ride a bull, make it a huge bull that you would have to climb a ladder to mount. You can justify it to the audience with your dialogue, but it will be fun to see what the other actors think you're doing.

As part of the second group, wipe your mind of anything as the game is starting. Don't try to guess what the scene is about; just follow the action and let it tell you a story. Then retell that story. It's smart for the second group to decide in advance which actor will replace which actor of the first group. That way you need to follow the actions of only one person through the scene.

Variation We also play a version of this called, "Hear No Evil; See No Evil." In this version, one actor can't see the scene, and the other can't hear it. Together they must try to make their version as close as they can to the original. This game teaches teamwork because one actor saw everything and the other heard all the dialogue. This gives them everything they need to do the scene, but they have to do it without giving too much direction to the other person. We do see a lot of interaction like, "Weren't you going to ask me to jump up and down?" or "I don't know why, exactly, but I think you should twist that large knob over there."

80 Understudy

For the emcee/teacher: In this game, the scene is replayed three times. The first is the setup scene by two actors where everything is perfect. It should run about 90 seconds. Meanwhile, keep two actors offstage where they can't see or hear what is being done.

As the scene concludes, you suddenly announce that an actor from the first group is ill and must drop out. Call for an understudy.

In the second version of the scene, one of the actors from backstage replaces the "ill" actor. The actor from the previous scene, still on stage, leads the scene again. When that scene is played for the second time, the remaining actor from the first scene falls ill. Call another understudy.

With the third version of the scene, one actor is brand new to the scene, and the other was led through it by an original actor. This game represents an actor's worse nightmare but fun things can happen as the actors try to make it work.

For the players: For this game to work, the "understudies" should come on with complete confidence. No matter what play title and scene the emcee announces, you, as the understudy, proclaim that you know it well. At no time should you look lost in the scene, even when you know you're way off base. (Instead point out that you played it differently in the cast you were in, putting the blame on the current troupe instead of yourself.)

81 Half-Life

For the emcee/teacher: Give the actors a scene and exactly one minute to complete it. At the end of one minute, have them set up again and do the entire scene again in half the time: 30 seconds. The scene then gets done again in 15 seconds, 7 seconds, and 3 seconds, and finally we see the entire thing set up in 1 second.

Help the actors by calling out time marks along the way. In the first scene, call the time left at 30 seconds, 15 seconds, and then give a 5-second countdown. This will guarantee that the actors go for a big ending, which is very important because it will be the same big ending in each version. Be sure to call out the 15-second point and the 5-second countdown in the 30-second scene. You can simply count down in the shorter scenes.

For the players: Consider a few tricks for making this game work. The first is that in the 1-minute scene, you should take your time. Don't rush it. This way, when you do the 30-second scene, it will flow naturally, and you won't miss a line or action. This will shock the audience because they won't realize that you really just stretched a 30-second scene into a minute in your first attempt.

Another element to use to your advantage is the third actor. The emcee will be calling the time at the halfway point in the first two scenes, so it's easy to know when you're in the middle of your scene. That's a great time to bring out the third player and give the scene a boost.

Finally, make sure the ending is big. This will help the very short scenes because you'll have an explosion of action. The 1-second scene should be just a clash of actors to get to the ending lock-up.

Variation This scene can be done in reverse to challenge the actors. Start with the 1-second "explosion" and then keep stretching the scene out to show what led to the big ending. This scene is very hard because you'll be amazed at how long 30 seconds can be when you don't know what needs to go there, and then the 1-minute scene will seem like an hour.

82 The Director

For the emcee/teacher: This game will have you acting like a film director. Establish a setup for a scene you are going to film and then call "Action." The actors will begin building the scene until you call "Cut." At this point, give each of them some sort of direction—an emotion, accent, occupation, motivation, etc.—that must be included when they perform the scene again. The actors reset the scene, you call "Action," and they replay it, adjusting for your new direction.

We usually do three "cuts" with the scene, and we build it as if the game is one long scene. For example, when "Cut" is called the first time, the director isn't feeling the scene and needs the actors to have more emotion. The audience helps assign a different emotion to each actor, and the scene begins again. The next time "Cut" is called, it's because the director needs the actors to change their motivation. The audience helps with that, too. The final "Cut" is called because the director has found out that the producer thinks the show needs more of an international flare and different accents will be assigned to each actor. The fourth scene is a remake of the first scene, but with actors each having a specific emotion, motivation (or occupation), and accent. It's great to see what actors can do with this. It helps if the first scene is kept small.

For the players: Bring all of your new endowments into the scene. The audience will be looking for you to add them one at a time, so do what you can to make that happen. Keep the scene intact throughout the craziness that will follow.

One other thing we like to do to keep the overall scene going is to have each actor become a different character when "Cut" is called. If you were a wimpy person in the scene you just did, be very tough between takes. This will help with the illusion of the "movie set" that you've created. You can use this character while the "director" is giving you another layer.

83   POV

For the emcee/teacher: The name of this game, "POV," stands for the film term "point of view." In the game, you'll have the actors perform a basic scene, but then have them perform it over again giving each actor a chance to present it from his or her point of view.

This game is fun to work out on stage. Each time the scene is replayed, the POV actor comes out the hero of the scene and the other actors suddenly play minor, supporting roles. Playing this game correctly will teach the actors how to step back (and step up) when needed.

For the players: Playing the hero of the scene is easy and fun. Just think about what you did in the first scene and do it bigger. If you brought someone a drink of water in the first scene, scale a mountain to bring water from a raging river in the next. Often the game becomes a competition to see who tops the other actors.

The real trick to the scene is playing the supporting roles. When you're the hero, it's easy to make it all about you, but in the other versions, you'll be doing the same actions in order to make the other person heroic. For example, in one scene you might make the decision to clip the red wire and defuse a bomb, but in the other you don't know what wire to cut and have to ask the hero. In both scenes you're clipping the wire, but the idea of who was the "hero" has changed.

Variation   There is a "Line-up" variation of this game that you can try with a small group of actors. Get a fairytale or other well-known story and assign each of the actors a part. Now you'll run the scene like "Talk Talk" (Game #60), but when you point to an actor, he will keep the story moving, but from his point of view. This doesn't necessarily mean that the story will be about the actor you've picked; it's just from his point of view. For example, the Woodsman in "Little Red Riding Hood" doesn't figure into the story until the end, but he might have witnessed something that we didn't know about. This is why we're hearing others' points of view.

84   Lone Survivor

For the emcee/teacher: Players perform a scene based on a suggestion from you or the audience. Something with action or emotion will work best here. When the scene is finished, remove one of the actors.

Have the remaining two actors play the scene again, re-creating with two everything that the three of them had done in the original scene. Explain to the actors that they should make sure that any information they added to the scene is still brought up, but it's as if the third actor had never been a part of it.

Next remove another actor. The "Lone Survivor" will then do a one-person scene based on what he or she learned from the other actors and the previous scenes. Done correctly, the closing scene will have the look of a dramatic monologue, usually a bad one. In fact, that's usually what we're going for at the end. It's our way of paying homage to those days at drama competitions.

For the players: Keep an eye on everything that is being done and said in the first scene. You should be doing that in every scene, but in this game, you'll need to know what will have to survive to the next scene in case you're the actor left standing.

85   The Impossible Scene

For the emcee/teacher: Okay, so it's not impossible. But it is hard to do this scene perfectly—so it's close to impossible.

The actors will do a scene based on an activity you give them. However, they must do it without saying "I," "me" or "my." That's tough, but not too bad. Next, they'll re-do the scene, but this time, in addition to the first-scene stipulations, they can't ask questions. Still pretty tough, but if they don't ask too many questions in the first scene, it's doable. In the final version, they can't say those certain words, can't ask questions, and now can't make any reference to the activity that they are doing. Now it's nearly impossible.

For the players: Keep your mind on the things you can't do; the audience will pounce whenever you make a mistake. Above all else, keep the scene going, but make sure that you're following the rules.

Variation Do this as a competitive game. A team loses points every time one of its players breaks a rule.

Bizarre Games

There is not much to be said about these games, other than that they are really strange and usually very popular with the audience. Some players will say these games are nothing but gimmicks, but I say that even a game like "Mousetrap" needs to have a scene at its base or it won't work.

A few of these games, or others brought up in the first book, break down quickly, so you have to build the scene quickly and try to stay with it. It's a lot like riding a bull. You get on, make sure the ropes are tight and that you've got a good grip, and then, when someone opens the gate, all you can do is just try to hold on until it's over.

86 Spit Take

Props Bottles of water

For the emcee/teacher: The players perform a scene based on the given suggestion. Each has a bottle of water that they drink nonchalantly during the scene. But whenever someone is "shocked," he spits the water in basic comic fashion. This "spit take" often takes place directly into the face of the person who spoke last.

This game is not for every actor. People who are squeamish about getting spit on by another person will not want to be a part of it, but for those who can handle it, this game is a lot of fun. Make sure it's the last game played because the stage is going to be covered with water when it's all over.

For the players: This game is all about the spit takes, so you don't have to actually be "shocked" to do the spit. But no matter what triggers the reaction, you should announce it with shock. As an example, if an actor comes up and asks if you've done your homework, you can do the spit take and then say, "What?! We had homework?" This is often said over the laughter of the crowd.

It's also fun to do the opposite. If someone gives you actually shocking news, you can swallow the water and say that you're not surprised at all. Obviously this is something that should be done sparingly so the joke doesn't get old, but it's a good way to add to the scene.

This is a game that you'll just have to play with to see what works for you.

87 Mousetraps

Props A lot of mousetraps; a blindfold for each actor

For the emcee/teacher: This game is a huge audience favorite but is not so well loved by the actors. We like to set it up as "Improv's Most Dangerous Game." Actors do a basic scene on a stage full of loaded mousetraps. And, they're doing this while barefoot and blindfolded. Yes, you read it correctly.

You need a good number of mousetraps to make this work. We work with at least 30 spread out, but more is better. Also make sure that you have good blindfolds. I like to use safety or swim goggles taped up (you can even draw eyes on them to add to the silliness). Once the actors are ready, lead them center stage and let them go to work.

Station other actors near the front of the stage to direct the actors back into the action and to make sure they don't fall off. These actors can also reset mousetraps that have snapped. As the emcee, call the game when you feel it has reached its peak.

For the players: There is a chance that you will feel a bit of pain in this game, but it's less than you might think. In fact, only about one out of six traps will actually get you, and only about one out of ten of those will hurt.

You will most likely step on a trap with your full foot. When you do that, just pull up quickly and the trap will shut with a loud "snap." The audience will see your reaction and think the trap got you. It's all in the reaction. Knowing this will help you get over any fear of the traps so you can do the scene. You can also let a few get you in the warm-up just so you know the worst that can happen.

I really stress a scene with this game. The easiest way to make this happen is each time you set off a trap, you have to come up with an explanation for the sound and your reaction that somehow relates to your scene. The explanation can be ants, gun shots, or even a hamstring snapping—whatever will fit the scene you are doing. After a while the scene will collapse into a lot of traps and frightened actors, but if you've set up a scene at the beginning, all is good. At this point the emcee will call the game.

88 Movie Pitch

Props A box of different pictures; a magnetic whiteboard; several magnets (or something else to post the images on)

For the emcee/teacher: The setup for this game takes a bit of work. You will need to find images that are big enough to be seen by the audience but not so big that they take over the board. I went to a "teacher's supply store" and bought a bunch of images they'd use for their classroom bulletin boards. You want a good mix of people, objects, locations, and animals.

The idea of the game is that the players are pitching a movie idea to the audience. They reach blindly into the box of images and pull images out one at a time, working whatever they find into the story. The actors put the images on the board so that they can be referenced as the scene continues and to remind the audience of what has been going on so far. Actors also may interact with the images from time to time, performing little scenes to help the pitch. The "pitch" should tell the entire story of the movie and should be told with a lot of energy and passion.

For the players: You've got to play this scene with total confidence. Your career depends on selling this movie!

Follow the three-act formula of a movie for this game. You set up the characters and the situation with the first act, bring in the conflict in the second act, and reach the resolution in the third. We've found it best if you use nine to twelve pictures total, dividing them up in the acts. This is very helpful because it reminds you to wrap up the act at a certain time. For instance, if you know you're going to use nine cards, you will wrap up act one with the third card and then start with the conflict on the fourth.

Lead into your story before you pick the cards. By "leading" I mean that you set up the card before you pick it out of the box. You might say, "We begin our story in a quiet, sleepy town, where we meet a..." and then draw the card. Who knows what you'll draw, but whatever it is, it's what you meet in that town. Your scene has begun. Or you could go into act two by saying something like, "But their peaceful existence is about to be rocked by the sudden appearance of..." and see what your conflict is going to be. This will help your story and be fun for the audience because your lead-ins will often build a strange plot line.

This is theater of the mind, so you won't have actors acting out a scene, but the scene is still there, on two levels. First you have the story that is being told, and since it's in a three-act setup, it should flow well. But you've also got the secondary scene of the actors making the pitch.

Variations

- This game makes for a great solo game where an actor does the scene alone.

- This format can be fun for a single scene or lead to the start of a long-form where the actors can take some of the themes of the pitch and run with them for the longer scenes.

89 Amish Rake Fight

For the emcee/teacher: If there is a more bizarre game than this, I don't know what it is. But it's become an audience favorite, so it's stuck around.

A group of actors are given a setup for a scene built around something that you would never expect the Amish to do...space travel, for example. The actors must now find a way to perform this scene as only the Amish could.

The other actors wait to the side of the stage, pretending to hold rakes. Whenever the actors on stage do something "against the Amish way of life," the side actors rush the stage, announcing the infraction and miming hitting them with the rakes.

That is basically it. It is a silly, silly game with a crazy name. I think the audience likes it just because they get to yell out "Amish Rake Fight!" I do need to point out that this game is not meant to offend the Amish in any way and that I would still feel good about playing it if there were Amish people in the crowd, but in almost 20 years of playing this game, that hasn't happened.

For the players: There are two groups here, so let's talk about the on-stage Amish first. You will need to take on the mannerisms and speech of this people, and, more importantly, you have to figure out how to do what the scene suggests. This can be very tough, but getting it worked out is very rewarding... like the time we made it to the moon by building a barn propelled by butter churns. Stay with the scene and characters and see what you work out.

The "Rake Holders" (who act like "keepers of Amish law") need to watch the scene and find the offenses. Some are easy to spot, like using electricity, but most of the Amish actors will know to stay away from that. You can look for some—"displaying pride" or "disobeying an elder"—but we mostly make up things that sound good. Over the years, we've made up rules that probably don't exist in the Amish culture, but we sold them as if they did. (And for all we know, they might.)

The "rake fight" should be quick so the scene can continue. Often one hit is enough. Also, don't forget to let the scene develop. The rake part is funny, but if it's constant, it will get old. And it's also just as much fun to watch a team of actors figuring out how to do something the "Amish way."

90 Ballet

Music Classical music suitable for accompanying a ballet performance

For the emcee/teacher: I talked about this game earlier in the book in one of my "Magic Moments of Improv." The idea is simple: The actors perform a scene by telling it only through ballet. Give them a situation that seems out of place in ballet (remember the NASCAR story?) and then let them go. Playing the right music behind them is key.

For the players: Don't worry about being a great dancer for this game; very few improvisers practice ballet. But watch some before playing to see some of the standard movements. Watch enough ballet, for example, and you'll see that someone dancing alone is either incredibly happy or devastatingly sad. There is no middle ground for a solo. And a two-person *pas de deux* is usually about love. Finally, some sort of tragedy almost always befalls one (or all) of the characters. Put all of that knowledge into what you're doing, and you'll have a great scene.

Be sure to overplay everything. Remember that you can't speak what is happening, so you'll have to have to sell every emotion. Watch a ballet in which someone cries or is sad: Their arms portray a lot of that emotion. Notice how the dancers will use the entire stage to show grief or happiness. You can do this, too.

Variation Play this with a narrator explaining the story as it unfolds. This person can both tell the story and lead it by announcing new characters before they appear on stage or getting the dancers to do certain things. The narrator should use soft tones of a PBS-type announcer. The whole thing can be done as a TV show where the "host" is going to show you a great ballet. We go back and forth as to which method we like the best.

91 Calling the Shots

Props Cardboard frames

For the emcee/teacher: In this game, you, as the emcee, will act like a movie editor and call different shots (medium, long, and close-up) for the actors to cut to during a scene. A "medium shot" is what you normally see on stage. For a "long shot," the actors will use their hands to represent their bodies (the middle and index fingers acting like legs). And the "close-up" is performed by using frames of different sizes, which will "frame" what you want to see in the "close-up." For instance you can use a small frame over an actor's eyes to show fear or concentration.

I suggest you check out some videos of an Australian comedy duo called the "Umbilical Brothers." They do some of this type of action in their stage shows. They also had a TV show called *The Upside Down Show* with a segment called "Action Fingers" that will give you more help.

You can do any type of scene here, but the actors will likely need an action-type setting so that the various shots will work. Look for the right moments to call the edit change. For example, if the actors announce that they're going to have to jump over something, go to a long shot and let them go to their hands to jump a long distance. A fight scene could use a lot of quick cuts to bring about great action.

For the players: Keep the scene going but make sure that what you're doing will help lead to cuts. You don't want to be in one shot too long. You'll find great ways to get to the long and close shots, and the medium shot is perfect for setting up.

Feel free to use some other items as well. If you're doing the big jump, you might want to use the backs of chairs as the different sides of the canyon. Children's toys can become motorcycles or horses for your fingers to ride.

The close-up can really work if you have multiple frames. If you take poster board and make different sizes of frames, you'll be able to do a close-up that is about two feet square and some that are super close, like just your eye. When you do the close-up, make sure to move to the front of the stage to make the close-up seem as real as possible.

Variation You can call out some other techniques such as "slow motion" to add to the scene. Find various movie techniques that can work for your group.

Long-Form

You can read my thoughts on long-form improv earlier in the book (see page 21). This form is a fun way to fully explore themes and characters. Everyone should try it.

Long-form types of improv have many different types of setups (it's hard to call them "games") but here are a few that I find a lot of fun. The last two, "Full-Length Play" and "Full-Length Musical," are my favorites and will need a fair amount of explanation (and even more rehearsal on your part).

92 Armando

For the emcee/teacher: This game (named after its creator Armando Diaz) was one of the first long-forms I ever did. It's still one of the easiest. One actor is given a theme by the audience and performs a monologue based on that theme. The actor can talk about anything she wishes within the theme, but she should try to explore it a bit within the 2- to 3-minute limit.

The other actors perform scenes based on what is talked about in the monologue. (I usually keep the monologue actor out of the other scenes.) They can explore the elements of what the monologue discussed but should stay close to what was actually said. The scenes need to come from the monologue and not just from the theme.

For the players: If you're presenting the monologue, give the players plenty to work with. Try not to make your monologue one simple story; add layers to it. Segue along different tangents so the players will have more content. But, of course, stay on theme.

If you're one of the scene players, listen closely to everything said. You don't need to do a strict reenactment of what you heard; your scenes should be based on the monologue's emotions and other elements.

Variation Have the monologue performer and the scene actors take turns. This way you get a monologue, some scenes, and then another monologue based on the scenes that were performed.

93 Following Shot

For the emcee/teacher: My improv troupe, Quick Wits, entered a long-from competition and surprised everyone by winning with a game we made up on the spot. This is that game.

The title comes from film. We start with two actors presenting a scene based on a theme you give them. After the scene is established, a third actor enters and interacts with them before making his exit. The next scene follows that third actor to his location, where he and another actor interact. The earlier pattern repeats as a third actor enters the scene; when she leaves, the scene follows her to her location, where another scene develops.

With this formula, you can create an entire town in which scenes can take place. Stories and characters intersect as your players begin to see this as a living, breathing form, not just a series of random scenes based off of a theme.

While not a traditional, explorative long-form, this game will surprise you as to the types of stories that can come from it. Plus it still allows you to grow a character and theme from beginning to end. In the end, you should have a front-to-back story told in one long take.

For large groups, this game can give everyone a chance to shine. It is fun to have each character "followed" to see what makes her tick. Don't be afraid to have the followed person go somewhere by herself for a little while; it's one way to see the character's inner workings. Then have someone come in to keep the movement going. For smaller groups, double up on characters. Make those who are leading the story more important, but use the others to help round out a story.

For the players: You can hone your storytelling skills. Keep watching what's developing on stage. If you've already introduced a character in this scene, try and see how he or she fits within what's happening. If you haven't developed a character yet, imagine what this story might be missing and add it in.

94 Clue

For the emcee/teacher: This is another long from we developed for a competition. Although it wasn't as successful as "Following Shot," it makes a great stage show.

Begin with all the actors in the same room. A murder has been committed, and the players will speak to a detective as they try to figure out who did it. This will be quite the trick; as of right now, no one knows who the victim is or how that person was killed. You'll get all of that—and anything else they might want to give—from the audience. Often you will play both the detective and the victim/host.

This is a game of setting up scenes by accusing other "guests." A character might say that she overheard a loud fight between the victim and one of the guests. As the accused explains what really happened, the other actors will perform the scene. That accused person then points a finger at another and that scene is acted out.

The scenes go back and forth usually until a specified time and then the ending is revealed. It usually falls to the detective to make the final accusation and then we hear the confession and sometimes see the murder acted out. The emcee/host role is fun because you're in a lot of the scenes, but mostly in bizarre ways. Play them all up, but don't tip your hand one way or the other as to who the killer is.

For the players: This is a murder mystery. Find a character for yourself and play it up. Find red herrings about yourself or the other actors. Someone playing this game to the hilt will have made it look like he is the killer but has already prepared a way to disprove that accusation.

Before long, you should be able to see where your character fits into things. You will need to make sure you have an alibi and can discredit those of the others. This game is truly "Yes, and" because you can't just say that someone was lying, you have to show how they were.

Keep looking for ways to make the others look as guilty as possible. The more you can deflect from yourself, the better, but do it within the context of the game. If someone says she saw you stab the victim, you have to show how you did that but didn't kill him. Another thing you can do is setup scenes that don't have the victim in them. You can create a scene where two of the other actors were heard plotting the victim's death. Now make them act that out and see what they do.

Variation You can involve the audience by letting them pick the killer. They've been watching everything and have made up their minds as to who they think is guilty. Have the detective collect their votes and look them over. Then the actors will go on stage and act out the ending. The guilty party will then have to come up with the full story as to why he or she did this foul deed.

95 Spoon River

For the emcee/teacher: This is a scene that plays out in monologue form. The actors line the stage and step out one at a time to tell their stories based on a theme given to them from the audience. Have each person introduce herself and give information about her character. From there, the story can be told through the actors' monologues.

The story includes all the elements of a scene but can be examined more through the thoughts of the actors involved. It needs to come across as different people all telling the same story, showing how they were affected by what happened.

For the players: This form can often break down into a scene between the actors if they're not careful. Remember that you're telling your side of the story and not interacting with the other actors. Listen to what they're saying and figure out how that impacts your character.

Also, be mindful that all characters need to have equal time in this game. Don't monopolize the scene because you think that you've got important things to say. Share the stage time.

Variation This game goes by many names (Goon River, Moon River, Spork River, etc.), but the variations are very slight. Find a way to make this game your own and give it a new name.

A short-form version of this game is easily played out by making the scene shorter. You can play the game as "Voices from Heaven": Have the actors tell stories of how they got to heaven with the twist being that they were instrumental in each other's lives somehow, and possibly their deaths.

96 RPG

Props A few 20-sided dice

For the emcee/teacher: "RPG," which is short for role-playing game, is based on this gaming foundation. Actors come up with their characters, introduce them to the audience, and roll a 20-sided die to determine a few things about their character. These rolls will give them their "Charm," "Strength," "Speed," and "Intelligence." The higher the roll, the better they are in that category.

Each character is given a quest that she must complete. The emcee/"Dungeon Master" will describe situations to the actors and interact with them. Through it all, you can have members of the audience roll dice to determine if they are successful in various tasks. Both successes and failures must be acted out.

The rules are up to the troupe. It will be up to you and your actors to decide how in-depth you want to go with your gameplay. For instance, you can decide how many "hits" a character can take before he is dead. Everything will be up to you, but make sure the audience knows the basic rules (usually by putting them in a program).

This game is best played in episodes. I've seen this performed successfully back East where troupes host a show once a week and crowds show up to see what happens. I was in a crowd one night when a popular character died, and I actually saw a few tears as the actor played out his death. I was amazed—and saddened that I was only in town for one show.

For the players: I'd say that knowing how to play a role-playing game will really help you. If someone in your troupe has experience with RPGs, let her take you through a game so you can see how they work. The way they are played around a table is pretty much the same as you'd play them on stage.

Be true to your character. This game will allow you to grow through the weeks, and you'll see how you might actually shed a tear when a character dies. And remember that the dice always have the final say. If they say you fail, you fail.

Variation This should really be its own game, but count it as a hidden bonus. We've played a version of "James Bond" movies where we get the mobile phone numbers from people in the audience and whenever we need something we will call a random number and get our next bit.

Let's say you want to know more about the villain you're supposed to meet. You call up the "headquarters" and ask them for some defining characteristic. The audience member's phone rings, he answers it, and you ask him. Whatever he tells you becomes a part of the bad guy's character. You can do a lot with something like this because it's fun for the audience to suddenly be drawn into the scene.

97 In the News

Prop A newspaper

For the emcee/teacher: Actors take a current newspaper and read some of the stories and headlines. They should each have different pages and sections so you get a good cross-section of events. All of this can be done in a "Hey, listen to this!" type of setup.

After enough stories have been told, have the actors act out scenes based on themes found in the stories. They don't need to act out exactly what they read, just whatever inspires them from the stories. This can be funny or sad: One of the best scenes I've seen was done after reading about a tragic car crash. The actors did a scene about a family dealing with it all. It was powerful and not at all what I was expecting.

For the players: Sometimes it's best to use the stories that aren't the "big headlines." Find the stories that have something unexpected to them. Make sure that the stories told are a good mix of themes. This isn't about finding one theme to tie them together; the theme is really "A Day in the Life of a Town," and you can only do that by telling the whole story.

Don't be afraid to examine hard things with this format. Most really good performances that I've seen in this form have had only a few laughs, and those came at cathartic moments. Use this format to boost your dramatic acting.

Variation Newspapers are good for this form, but you can use different mediums as well. Ask the audience for inspirational stories from their lives and go from there. Remember to get a good mix from them as well. The crowd will bond over this version because they are sharing some of themselves with you. Don't mess that up by going for cheap laughs.

98 Harold

For the emcee/teacher: The "Harold" is often looked at as the granddaddy of improv. Created in the late 1960s by Del Close, it is also referred to as a 3 × 3 scene because its basic format is three different scenes shown in three segments each.

A lot of material—including entire books—exists about this format. I'll give an overview of a "Harold"; you decide if it's something you'd like to dive into more deeply.

As I mentioned, a "Harold" has three scenes as its basis. This will play out in the structure below:

Opening
Scenes 1a, 2a, 3a
Group Game
Scenes 1b, 2b, 3b
Group Game
Scenes 1c, 2c, 3c

The "Opening" segment can be done in different styles. It can be a song, monologue, or any type of scene that sets a frame around the theme for the Harold. Troupes can experiment with different openings but its main purpose is to help announce "the theme."

Now we have the first three scenes. Each will include two to three actors and will be unrelated to the others. The actors can use some of the details from the opening game to create their scenes.

This is followed by a group game where the actors get together and perform. Many different types of games can be played here, but they should flow with the theme and involve everyone. Different troupes have their thoughts about the "break" games so work with your actors and see what fits with your style. It's best to think of these breaks as almost a commercial between the scenes. They let time pass for the three scenes, entertain the audience, and keep the actors engaged.

Now you'll do the second group of scenes. Looking back at "Movie Pitch" (Game #88), you'll see that I divided that game into three sections (introduction, conflict, and resolution). You can do the same sort of thing in a Harold. That would mean that in this third scene the stakes are raised, and we have a conflict that our characters will have to handle. Another hook for the second scene can be a long passage of time since the first scene. As an example, in the first scene a baby can be born, but in the second scene, the child is now twenty-five and still won't move out of the house. Make sure that your scene grows with this second installment.

Now we have the second Group Game break. It's best if this game is very different from the first.

The end of the Harold is the resolution of the scenes. This can be all three scenes hitting their resolve, or some of the scenes combining; it's up to the actors and the flow of things. This ending should also be the shortest of all the scenes; sometimes it's nothing more than a stinger (a short scene of only a few lines). In the example of our married couple with the stay-at-home son, the parents can be in heaven finally enjoying themselves when the son arrives, saying that he missed them.

A Harold usually runs between 30 and 45 minutes. The form is often used by troupes to either start or end a show. This format will work well for troupes that are mixing long and short-forms because it is basically a group of short scenes and games mashed together.

For the players: Take some time working through the format. Troupes that have been doing this for a long time don't plan out any part of it. But when you're doing it for the first few times, you might want to have a few things mapped out. For instance, you might work out what games you're going to play during the breaks, or you might decide which actors are going to work together in the scenes and which order they are going to be performed. This will help you get a handle on the Harold.

Variation Obviously your troupe can play different games during the breaks, but you can vary the form itself. Troupes have done this in a "reader's theater" style as if it were a radio play. It's also been done with all the actors acting out their scenes in the same location, with different outcomes. And you can also do a Harold without the between-scene games. As with all improv, figure out what works for your troupe.

99 The Exhibit

Props As dictated by your "exhibit"

For the emcee/teacher: This is an experimental form. The idea is that the audience has been invited to an exhibit of some sort. This can be an art show of whatever medium you'd like, or even something like a debate or town meeting. Anything that gets people together and offers a chance for mingling will work.

The actors will be different characters in the meeting. These actors will be given only a name and a role (artist, critic, assistant, etc.). The rest will be up to them and the audience. They will also be given some sort of identifying mark so that the audience will know that they are part of the show.

As the audience arrives, each person will be given a slip of paper that she can give to any of the actors. On these slips, people will write instructions to the actors, telling them what the audience members want them to do. These instructions can be anything from "Cause a scene" to "Kiss an audience member" to "Admit to murder." The idea is that no actor will know what he is going to get throughout the night or how that will start to craft a story.

The audience will have a fun time controlling the actors and seeing the results played out against the big picture. The show can have a time limit or you can see if an ending comes naturally. I find it best if you work toward both. Know the time you want to end it and have the actors work their way to a climactic ending.

For the players: You have no idea what will be given to you, so don't try to force anything too early. Just play out your part and wait for the audience to make its move. Then once you start getting your orders, figure out what they mean. Remember that you're likely to get a few things, and you'll have to work them all into your character.

Whatever you do, make sure that it's big enough for everyone to see (unless the order was something more private). The other actors will need to see what you're doing so that they know how to use their orders. And always keep in mind that this show is for the audience; they will want to feel as if they've controlled the evening. So don't go too far off the path and be ready for anything.

Variation This can be a nice fund-raiser type of show. Think about putting it around a silent auction or dinner where people are already thinking about donating. Then you can actually sell the "orders" to people who want to donate. Let them give you more money, and you can give them a blank slip on which they can write their own order. Just make sure that everyone knows that you have to approve the order. You don't want things getting too out of hand.

The exhibit can be a change of pace for people who are tired of seeing the same old murder mystery played out at a dinner party. This way, they will have a bigger hand in deciding the show, instead of just trying to guess the killer.

100 Fully Improvised Play

Doing full-length plays and musicals is easily my favorite part of improv. I'm going to lay out some thoughts and ideas for this section, but know that when I get a new group of people together for full-length improvisations, we will practice for several weeks. The idea is to make it look easy, but it will take a lot of work and trust.

Crafting the Story

The first thing to work on is how to recognize story structure. Unless you just opened this book, you've heard me talking about the main ideas in a scene and story: introduction, conflict, and resolution. These three elements will come into play when putting together a show like this. That shouldn't surprise you. Every character is going to need to be introduced to the audience, will need a reason (conflict) to exist and interact with others, and will need to bring it all to a conclusion.

The first step is always the introduction. Within a few lines, you will need to establish your basic character. You don't have to go too deep at first; just say who or what you are. This is very easy to do, and the audience won't think it forced because it happens in every show. Sometimes this comes from the other actors who might call you by your title (Mom, Mayor, Custodian). If that happens, let's hope that what they say is who you are hoping to play.

The first scene in a new location will also need to have something to let the audience know where they are. You may not have programs or fancy sets to communicate this information, but you don't have to say, "Here we are in a factory" to do this. Simply go through the motions of working in a factory and talk about work. Creating your environment through movement becomes even more important in this format.

Conflict can now start to develop. Be careful not to bring it on too soon. The second scene is probably the earliest to begin developing one of the conflicts. Before this can happen, you'll need to establish your protagonists and antagonists (heroes and villains). It's important that every actor recognize who is filling these roles and not stray from them.

Since we're coming up with plots out of nowhere, it's best to stick with basics, so creating a conflict should be easy. Once you know who the hero is, find out what her dream is and go squash it. If she's just opened a business, shut it down. If she is looking for love, stop it. You get the idea. It's simple, but simple is what will help you in the beginning.

Then you will need to work out how the story will end. It's pretty clear that you'll want the good guys to come out on top (or do you?) so it's just a matter of finding the right way to make it happen. The motivations of both the hero and villain should give you a clear path.

Secondary Plots

All of the above will give you a main plot, but your story should have more than that. Look at every play, movie, or book, and you'll notice secondary plots that fill up the story. What was *Harry Potter* about? You'll find that a lot of little things ran through each book, and many of them didn't concern Harry. Just watch a half-hour sitcom and you'll see that more than one plot carries an episode.

Secondary plots are just as important as the main one. While they may not be the main driving point of the play, they are very important to the characters involved in them. It's all about perspective.

Look for things that other characters can do. Some of them will want to help the hero achieve his goal, but even then it's okay to have other interests. Love is one of the biggest plot devices in storytelling, so if it's not the main plot, find two people to be the show's romantic interests. If love is the main plot conflict, then see what else is out there. What motivates some of the other characters? What are their dreams? Since the villain isn't targeting them, their dreams are even easier to obtain.

Communication

Now that I've said you have to come up with main and secondary plots on the spot, you're probably wondering how you do this. The simple answer is by talking to each other. You're not on the stage the whole time, so you'll have time to say a few things to the other actors about what you're thinking. A group will come to a consensus pretty quickly because fear and survival are great motivators.

The show will have to start with at least one person on the stage, and that character will be set pretty quickly. Others will enter the scene, and, as they're talking, the plot will develop. The people offstage will need to pay attention to this and work out where they think the scene could go. Don't try to map out the full show at this point but start to gather ideas.

The back-and-forth communication while the scenes are played out will be important. Often, you'll be discussing things that will involve the actors who are on stage. You'll need to make sure that they are told what you were discussing offstage. And they are likely to have ideas they were thinking while onstage.

This is why you can't try to come up with the full plot in the first scene. Everyone will need to have a say in this. Make sure that everyone is aware of what's happening and that the outline is very clear. But here is the kicker: You can't talk too much offstage because you still need to pay attention to what is happening. And at times, you might not have a chance to talk about your plan; you just have to "show" people in a scene. Several times, I've just grabbed someone and said, "I've got an idea. Come do a scene with me."

Talking It Through in Warm-Up

I know that all of this can get a little confusing and overwhelming, but it does start to stick with time. Before you start doing full scenes, I'd suggest sitting down with your troupe and giving them a topic for the play. Then let someone say how she would start it and what character she would be. She and/or the others can then determine what other characters would be in that scene and what it would accomplish. Then talk about what elements would be in the next scene and the characters involved. By now, everyone should have an idea of the plots available, and they can decide which they will play out. Now just talk through the scenes that would be needed to make all of this happen.

Talking through the show a few times will let actors see how it comes together and how the "group mentality" functions in this game. Be careful to watch out for people who are trying to lead the whole thing when you do it, or those who always set their characters up for lead roles. Get them to back off. The same can be said of actors who are always falling back to support roles. Ask them what they think and engage them in the discussions.

And I want to point out that I'm talking about this as an exercise not connected with the show. This is only to get you familiar with how to quickly see the elements of a story. You will find that this practice pays off greatly, however, when you're scrambling to get the plot going.

The Canadian Cross

This one is a little tough for actors, but in shows like this, you really need to have a few people who can play the smaller parts that might be needed in a scene. This could be the bellman at the hotel, the lifeguard at the beach, or any other situation in which you need a line or an action. This calls for a Canadian Cross.

In improv, a Canadian Cross is when an actor crosses the stage, usually coming on and off without interacting with the other actors, just to add more substance to the scene. Such characters add atmosphere but aren't meant to be a focal point of the scene. Sometimes they'll say a line, but more often than not, they are just background. In short-form this is most often played for laughs.

In a full-length play, these actors play characters who are important to a scene but maybe not to the overall story. A bartender to whom people tell their problems or a doctor who has to give the bad/good news are good examples. In a show, assign one or two actors to take on the duties of a Canadian Crosser and let them play multiple characters. At times, as the "Crosser," I ended up with more stage time than the leads.

Scene Layout

I find it helpful to follow a little pattern the first few times you play. This will help keep you focused and on track. Here is very basic scene layout:

> Opening Scene: Establish location and protagonist.
> Second Scene: Establish antagonist and possible conflict.
> Third Scene: Introduce support characters and secondary plot.
> Fourth Scene: Protagonist and antagonist are aware of their roles in the conflict.
> Fifth Scene: Minor plots are addressed.
> Sixth Scene: Major conflict comes to a head and plans are made.
> Seventh Scene: Resolution.

A quick seven-scene layout like this will work well for a 30-minute show. As you become more familiar with the form, you'll find that you can do many more scenes and establish more plots. You will also develop a scene order that works best for you. For a show that's an hour or longer, you'll want third- and even fourth-tier plots.

You can vary the length of your scenes. If you need only a minute or so to get your point across, don't pad it, just do what you need and move on. It may sound strange, but in longer shows it's actually better to do a lot of smaller scenes. Think about it like a movie—there are several cuts to keep the story moving. Your show should be like that.

Ending Scenes

You can end a scene many ways. The main thing is to have the ending make sense. Natural endings can take place with your dialogue. Think of shows that you've seen and how the scenes end. Usually the characters make a statement about what they're going to do or where they're going to go. Actors walking off a stage and leaving it bare is definitely a clue that the current scene is over.

Some actors are a little afraid to do this because they don't know if the other actors are ready. Don't worry about that because you need to focus on your scene. If it's over, just make your way offstage and let the others worry about getting the next scene going. But you can also take peeks offstage and see if the next group is ready to come on.

I find it best to end your scenes yourself. The opposite of this is the next scene coming on stage and "wiping" you off. This is usually a good hint that you went too long with your scene.

In theaters where you can control the lights, have someone dim them as the scene ends. If you get in a good rhythm with your technical improviser, you can have her end the scenes and possibly even play a little scene-change music.

The Show

Come up with the way that you want to start the show. I like to talk to the audience and get a few stories from them: embarrassing moments, great vacations, or whatever comes to mind. These stories often inspire the show you're about to do, and the crowd will love seeing these stories come to life.

Then I ask for a show title and a location that is central to our play. Have the actors ask for a few details that are special to their characters (a secret, an obsession, news that they're waiting to hear, etc.), and they can work these in. With these things in place, we're ready to begin.

Earlier I had mentioned that you usually don't have much of a set for the show, but that doesn't mean that you can't have some chairs or small props that you can bring onstage to make it seem bigger. The same can be said for wardrobe. A few pieces of clothing that can easily be added to existing clothing (a jacket, for example) can help set a scene quickly.

Theme

It's not unheard of to have a theme for your show already chosen before it begins. Letting the audience know that you're going to do a sci-fi or murder mystery won't take away the improv aspect of the show. You're still going to have to build the show, only now you have something resembling a foundation to put it on.

If you're going to do a theme, the first thing you should do is have your actors study the genre and the themes prevalent in it. Before the show, talk about the things you've discovered so that everyone is on the same page. You'll be amazed how that little bit of conversation beforehand will start to fall into place as the scene begins.

This is also a great place to use costumes and some scenery. With a known theme, you can have a nice backdrop in place or some period furniture ready to go. Costumes can also be ready to go if you know a basic time frame or theme. I've also been in themed shows where we have the audience bring props that they think will fit the theme. We then use them through the show, and the crowd loves seeing their objects on stage.

The key to a themed show is to make sure that you stick with it to the end.

Working Up to a Big Ending

Set a time limit for the show and decide if you want to break it into two acts or keep as just one act. The amount of time is completely up to you, but having it set will be another thing that helps to keep your actors in line.

As you do more of this format, you'll get a feel for how long an average scene will take. Now you can watch the clock and work out how much time you have left to tell your story. You will be able to break out the scenes and even let the actors know if they need to keep them short or lengthen them.

Everything should lead to an ending that wraps up the story. Make sure that you don't leave any of the secondary plots hanging. I find it best when the ending has been alluded to earlier in the show. An example of this would be to mention some sort of event (contest, harvest, wedding) that takes place in a few days or to say that something (rent paid, weapon destroyed, murderer revealed, etc.) has to be done. Making a statement in the first two scenes about an event or act that has to take place will show the actors the finish line, and they can start running toward it.

Don't Freak Out

The idea of doing a full-length play is very intimidating to most actors, especially those who have been doing mostly short-form, but if you follow the storyline from beginning to end, you'll do just fine. After a few rehearsals, you'll be knocking out plays in no time. And don't be surprised if you'd rather do this style over any others.

101 Fully Improvised Musical

Music Live accompaniment (see the Note on page 86)

It would be easy for me to tell you to just do everything that you would do in an improvised play and just add music. If you follow the rules laid out in the above game and go through the steps found in the music section of this book, you'll be able to put together a decent musical. Here are a few other tips that will help make your musical pop.

The Show Setup

Nearly everything that you did to get ready for an improvised play will be the same here, so the real difference comes in the show itself. Just as a regular play and a musical have differences, you'll find the same is true here.

It starts at the beginning when you're talking to the audience. You can do the same sort of information gathering as you would for a play, but you're going to want to get specific on a few things. Ask the audience for the title of the "hit song" from this musical and possibly another song. I make the second song a duet, but if you have a particularly daring cast, you can go with a "big dance number."

Now that your actors know two of the songs that need to be sung as well as the title, a setting, and a few other tidbits, the musical should come together. And, just like the play, you can work in theme shows. A "Rogers and Hammerstein" (the duo behind *South Pacific, Oklahoma, The Sound of Music*, and many more)-themed musical is perfect for most audiences. You can use the types of songs and story flow from famous musical writers to help you.

The Opening Number

A musical should open with a big number that sets the tone of the show. For the improvised musical, you can open the show with a number that introduces the audience to the location or theme of the show. This can be just one actor taking the stage and singing to the audience in a narrator style.

You can also use the opening number to introduce the cast, giving everyone a line or two to spell out who they are. This is fun but a bit risky. Since you haven't really got much going onstage yet, it's hard to know what roles need to be filled. But I have seen this work well, usually on theme nights where some stereotypes are well known.

One fun method to try in this opening scene is having each actor in his own "space" singing about his character, goals, dreams, etc. This is a modern musical setup and can be quite effective. To do this, let each have a verse on his own and then, when everyone is done, launch into it all over again, but this time with everyone singing. If you have a really large cast, keep it to the leads or a few actors.

Ending a Scene in a Musical

Many of the scenes you perform should either end with a song or soon after a song. Again, this is standard in many musicals. The reason is that once you've done a great song, it's best to move on. Let the accompanist play some of the music during the scene change, and the audience will be happy. You can add a few lines after the song, but don't try to go too far.

Of course at times you might have a second song in a scene, but these are rare in this format. An example of a second song would be for a scene to begin with someone singing (perhaps a song hoping for something to change) and then end with a different character singing a version of the same song with the same sort of theme. This is almost like a reprise.

Working with Your Accompanist

Finding the right person, or band, to handle your music is very important. They will need to have a good grasp of both how a musical works and how the people in the troupe like to function. Be sure to work with them as much as possible so that there is a give and take in the music. A good accompanist can get to the point that he knows where the singer is going and will hit just the right notes.

You can also have your accompanist play some background music from time to time in the scene. This often leads to a song and give hints to the style that the accompanist is thinking about using in the scene. It's a fine line, but one worth walking if your players are good enough.

Remember the Story

Don't get too wrapped up in the musical side of things. There is still a story to be told, and it can get lost if all the songs are "clever fluff." Make sure that you use your songs to further the story. You can sometimes make this work with a sing-speak style of song. Remember Professor Higgins in *My Fair Lady*? His singing was more of a way to tell the story with music in the background. If you find you need to tell more story, this is a way to do it.

And remember that the time for your story is going to be cut down by the songs. This means that you need the scenes to get to the point more quickly. Also, many of your scenes will end with the song, so you'll need to get to those plot points before the song starts.

End Big

Another musical tradition is to end the show with a big song, and you're going to want one to bring your show to a close. The song should wrap up everything and involve as much of the cast as possible. This way you can have it work as a curtain call.

It's good if you can work a few things into the closing song. One would be the title of the show. The audience loves it when the actual title they gave you shows up in song. Another thing would be to give the actors a chance to sing a verse of their own to wrap up their story or talk about where their character is heading. The closing song can also act as a moral for the story.

With everything going on, I would suggest that the closing song is more of a ballad, a slower song that can build. This will give the cast a chance to come together without the worry of having to work with a fast song. The chorus should also be easy enough for everyone to sing with the main part of it repeated a few times as the cast closes the show. You get the cast in a line at the end, singing together and raising their arms, and you'll get an ovation from the crowd.

If you opened the show with the "everyone singing at once" style, you can have the show end the same way. This can be a very powerful ending and bring the show full circle, which will really amaze the crowd since you were just making it up the whole time.

Know Your Musical and Have Fun

If everyone is locked into the components that are in a musical and sticks to the story, everything will work out well. Don't get too hung up on one part not working the way you want it. You'll find that the crowd is very forgiving of a wrong note or a missed rhyme. They know that what you're doing isn't easy.

In fact, when you tell the crowd that you're going to improvise a musical, many will think that it's impossible. The secret, like any good magic, is that it's easier than it looks, and it's all about showmanship. The easier you make it look, the more amazed they will be, and the more fun you will have.

Alphabetical List of Games

List of Games Arranged by Specific Categories

Games for Beginners

1 Devo
2 Five Things
3 Chinese Proverb
4 Barney
6 Samurai
8 Yes, Let's!
11 No, You Didn't
12 What Happens Next?
13 Sybil
14 ACE

15 Revolver
20 Scene with a Soundtrack
21 A to Z
23 Character Motivation
36 Driver's License
44 One-Word Debate
52 Scenes from a Hat
59 Connect the Dots
60 Talk Talk
82 The Director

Games for Intermediate Players

5 Ninja
7 Shootout
9 Alliteration
16 Overactors Anonymous
17 Infomercial
18 Movie Mad Lib
19 Michael Bay History
22 Acronyms
24 Family Dinner
25 Opposites
26 Soothsayer
27 Not This but That
28 Marriage Counselor
30 Bong. Bong. Bong.
31 Between the Texts
32 Sound Effects
33 The Newlywed Game

34 Dating Game
37 Human Prop
38 Big, Bigger, Biggest
39 Double Feature
40 Flashback
41 Heckler Battle
42 Jip-Parody
43 Kangaroo Court
46 Singles Bar
47 Top That!
48 Five Seconds or Die!
49 Hitchhiker
50 Town Hall
51 Rap Battle
53 Catchphrase
54 Caruso
55 Dance Craze

Games for Advanced Players

Games Not Requiring Props

Games Not Requiring Music

About the Illustrator

Trevor Robertson makes pictures and lives in Utah. He has illustrated posters, flyers, programs, cartoons, coloring books, buttons, logos, portraits, comics, and other assorted riff-raff for Thrillionaires Musical Improv Theatre, Grassroots Shakespeare Company, Grassroots Shakespeare London, Mortal Fools Theater Project, Utah Valley University, and other such folk. He does freelance drawing and design commissions and posts all of his cool pictures on his website www.trevordraws.com.

9 780897 936521